CHRISTIANITY

A Clear Case of History

Christianity

A Clear Case of History

A Study in Christian Evidences

Edward C. Wharton

3117 North 7th
West Monroe, Louisiana 71291

The purpose of Howard Publishing is threefold:

***Inspiring** holiness in the lives of believers,

***Instilling** hope in the hearts of struggling people everywhere,

***Instructing** believers toward a deeper faith in Jesus Christ,

Because he's coming again.

Christianity: A Clear Case of History
© 1977 by Howard Publishing
All rights reserved.

Published by Howard Publishing Co., Inc.
3117 North 7th Street, West Monroe, LA 71291-2227

No part of this publication may by reproduced in any form without the prior written permission of the publisher except in the case of brief quotations within critical articles and reviews.

Printed in the United States of America

First Printing 1977
Revised 1991

ISBN# 1-878990-09-8

Scripture quotations not otherwise marked are from the American Standard Version, ©1901 Thomas Nelson & Sons, ©1929 International Council of Religious Education.

TO

My wife Martha,
whose abiding faith
has often sustained me.

CONTENTS

FOREWORD

by
Avon Malone

The faith of the Christian does not hang from a skyhook. Authentic faith is not a blind, irrational leap into the dark. God has revealed himself in the blood and bone of human history. Faith is a rational step into the light, resting on reliable evidence.

Ed C. Wharton, able teacher and adept writer, brings the historicity of Jesus Christ to life with his clear, cogent presentation of convincing historical evidence. In addition to the inspired records of his life and works in scripture, Mr. Wharton brings before his reader the testimony of ancient historians—Tacitus, Seutonius, Josephus, and others—as they bear record to the historical reality of Jesus.

From that solid base the case for his deity and Messiahship is convincingly developed. The central proposition of John's gospel is the theme that pervades this splended work "Jesus is the Christ, the Son of God" (John 20:30, 31).

An excellent student and teacher of the biblical text, Ed Wharton has long had a consuming interest in Christian evidences. This book grows out of years of study in the field. It can be an immense help in equipping the reader "to give answer to every man . . . concerning the hope that is in you" (1 Peter 3:15). I commend this book and its able author in the hope that both might be widely used in the defense of “the faith that was once for all delivered to the saints.”

Avon Malone
Oklahoma Christian University of
Science and Arts
October 1, 1991

FOREWORD

by
The late Dr. Batsell Barrett Baxter

Pendulums have a way of swinging to extremes, and in our generation the pendulum is clearly swinging away from faith in God and respect for his inspired word. The trend is toward atheism or humanism.

The higher criticism so prominent in the nineteenth century and the liberalism of our own century have laid the foundation for the undermining of orthodox Christian faith. The Bible has been attacked and its credibility lessened by theologians and other religious leaders—the very men who should have defended its inspiration and authority.

While paying lip service to the moral and ethical principles found in the Bible, and while using the traditional religious words without their time-honored meanings, these men have been openly questioning the historicity and the authenticity of the Bible.

No wonder, with these views widely taught for a number of years, we are now reaping the fruit of such anti-religious influences. The man in the street, especially our youth, no longer respects the authority of the Bible. This drift away from faith in God is resulting in a widespread decline in ethics and morals and a general self-indulgence and license in regard to drinking, the use of drugs, sex and the like. Society is becoming less and less spiritual and more and more secular and materialistic. There is a growing decline in all aspects of respect for authority, and sacred institutions, such as marriage, are breaking down. Crime is also rising alarmingly.

What can be done about a world rushing headlong to destruction? The answer lies in calling men back to faith in God and in his Son Jesus Christ. Men must again respect the sacred Scriptures and desire to live righteously.

But how can so huge an undertaking be accomplished? Part of the answer lies in solid, thoughtful, faith-building writing such as we find in this present volume. All who read this book will be grateful to Ed Wharton for his fine presentation of firm evidence to support the authenticity of the Bible and the factuality of its record of history, as well as the authoritativeness of its moral and ethical principles.

It is refreshing to read such statements as, "Our purpose in this book is to point modern man back to the only real evidence there is for Christ—the evidence of the eyewitnesses themselves as it is preserved for us in the New Testament documents." The author demonstrates in a very convincing way that "the New Testament is not a compilation of mythical stories . . . (but) records the activities of real people and of actual events."

Among the twelve chapters which make up the book, the reader will find the opening chapter, "Jesus and History," very helpful, especially in its quoting of a number of extra-biblical sources concerning the actuality of Christ's existence. Valuable, too, are the two chapters dealing with the historical reliability of the New Testament. These are convincingly handled and are crucial to the believability of all of Christianity.

The four chapters on the resurrection of Christ are closely and convincingly reasoned from the accounts given in the New Testament. The reader is likely to discover new and important evidence among old and familiar passages.

The chapter on miracles condenses the evidences for the believability of miracles to a very small space—yet the case is convincingly made. The chapter on Christ's death has interesting, even new, points to consider. The book closes with further evidence on its central theme—the factual, historical nature of the evidences supporting the Christian religion. Also, in closing, the author shows how unbiblical is the modern tendency to base religious faith on subjective, emotional feelings.

All in all, the book serves a fine purpose. The chapters are well written in a clear, understandable style. More important, the evidence for Christian faith is solid. This is the kind of book that will help the pendulum, now swinging away from orthodox Christian faith, to reverse its direction—to return to that which is truth.

Ed Wharton is a man of much experience. He has preached the gospel of Christ for over three decades and has been a teacher of men who are preparing themselves to preach. He received his academic training from Abilene Christian University and Lubbock Christian College. He is married and has four children. The Whartons are a fine Christian family, a further evidence for the Christian faith in these times of general family failure. Christ's way is not only the true way in logic and reason; it also works.

Christianity: A Clear Case of History is a needed book. It will help many to find Christian faith and others to deepen their Christian faith.

The late Dr. Batsell Barrett Baxter
Onetime Chairman, Bible Department
David Lipscomb College
Nashville, Tennessee

PREFACE

It is very satisfying to witness a new interest in historical evidences for Christianity. Serious and inquiring people want to know if the Christian religion is hoax or history. This is apparent, not only from the new literature, but from a very personal vantage point. In my annual seminars in Europe and Asia, the most enthusiastic response—from all age levels and from non-Christian religions—results from teaching on the totally reliable history of the Christian faith exactly as presented in the New Testament. That includes evidence for Christ's miracles, his phenomenal death on the cross, his bodily resurrection, and the coming of the Holy Spirit to the apostles. In addition, there are hundreds of requests to our extension school for tapes of sermons and class lectures on the newly-developed course on historical Christian evidences. Our resident student body is composed of men and women from all walks of life, from college age to retirement age, and they come to us crying for a confirmation of the reality of Christianity.

It has been said that this is a "new approach" to proving the claims of the Bible, that we are pioneering a new course in the field of Christian evidence. But this is not the case. This kind of evidence for Christianity is nearly two thousand years old. It is precisely the approach which the apostles used to prove the resurrection claims for Christ. It is the approach of Matthew, Mark, Luke, and John in presenting reliable, verifiable, and convincing evidence. The New Testament writers made no arguments from science or philosophy for the divine nature of Jesus. Neither did they seek to convince men by their subjective feelings. But in the calm and objective style of men who knew from personal, eyewitness experience (as the apostles) and from painstaking research (by Luke) that what they were recording were the facts in the case, they wrote their accounts in the verifiable context of history for our serious consideration. Historical evidences for Christianity began with the apostles. This is *their* case for belief.

In point of fact, the case for belief in Jesus as the Son of God cannot be found in science or philosophy. It is a historical matter and must be investigated from the only historical sources in our possession—the New Testament writings. No observations on Jesus or the Christian system can be developed without that historical basis which the New Testament alone offers. It is essential, therefore, that the New Testament be received as a certified document of reliable history. The Christian religion is not simply a moral code; it is belief in Jesus as God who has the power to redeem us from sin, to raise the dead, and to judge the world for its ungodliness. The burden of proof for this extravagant claim lies squarely on the historic life and resurrection of Jesus as stated in the New Testament. The New Testament, then, must be viewed as a reliable record of facts in order to provide a credible ground of evidence for belief.

In this book, I have attempted to provide sufficient reasons (not all of them by any means) for accepting the New Testament as reliable history and to keep it from being theologically heavy. It is written for those who know little or nothing of the Bible, but who want to take a serious look at its claims. First, I have tried to make it clear that the New Testament is as reliable as any document of history. Then, by an appeal to those recorded facts of history, I have made an effort to systematically reproduce the logic of the apostles' own evidence for believing in Jesus as Lord and Saviour. By this means, we will rediscover the real power of the gospel in the first century and the reason behind the apostles' success in presenting it to a pagan world.

Christianity is not merely good advice for successful living. It is, as pointed out, belief in Jesus who will raise the dead to eternal judgment. Christianity is an altogether different way of believing and living because of Christ and his resurrection. And the proof of the Christian doctrine lies in the historic reality of his own life and resurrection. Any definition of Christianity which does not include these supernatural and redemptive aspects in a truly historical framework, reduces the death of Jesus to a meaningless sentiment, robs it of any real power to change men's lives, and makes it at best only another ethical system from the outdated past. Christianity's power to invade lives and turn them around is easily seen to rest on its historical reality exactly as it comes to us from the New Testament.

This is an effort to provide confidence in that reality and knowledge of the apostolic use of the evidence for Christ which is based on the facts of history. It is written with the hope that the full significance of what Matthew, Mark, Luke, John, Peter, and Paul preached and wrote—which is what we now call historical Christian evidences—will become common knowledge among those who seek to know the certainty of Christianity.

Edward C. Wharton
Sunset School of Preaching
Lubbock, Texas

1

Jesus and History

That a few simple men should in one generation have invented so powerful and appealing a personality, so lofty an ethic and so inspiring a vision of brotherhood, would be a miracle far more incredible than any recorded in the Gospels.

—Will Durant

Christianity in a Space-Time Dimension

Christianity is a historic religion. That means that it began and took shape at a particular time and place which can be located and verified in the framework of our historical past. Examining the evidence from history is an exciting and sound way to prove the claims of the Christian faith. At the close of one of my classes, a student gave me a book in which he had inscribed his gratitude for having learned the value and makeup of the historical context. His gratitude was due to his newly-acquired knowledge of the verifiable nature of history. He had just learned that there are documents of history, like those of the Bible, which can be verified to have recorded actual happenings in a real space-time dimension. There are records from the past which we have every reason to believe are true since both archaeology and contemporary documents from the same time zone have confirmed their general reliability. The student found that he could now go back into the past with a great deal of confidence. This became very meaningful to him when he observed for the first time that the New Testament was written in the same way—in the context of history. To him, the thought that Christianity was historical, not merely doctrinal, was a new idea altogether. It was a new and exciting discovery. Many, unfortunately, have yet to make that discovery.

"Toothless" Christianity

A widespread concept of Christianity currently advocates that we can be Christians without believing in a historical Christ. This approach to religion is reminiscent of Julian Huxley's approach to God. Huxley did not believe in God, but recommended that we get along better with each other when we believe there is a God. The Christian religion without Christ would be much the same; it would offer only the ground rules by which we would be governed. Whether Jesus actually lived is not important to this philosophy since the thing that really counts is the Christian ethic, which, at least in theory, is supposed to bring out the best in our relationships with each other.

Does it really matter whether Jesus actually lived and was divine? Be assured that it does. Passionate human beings cannot be motivated to live morally without believing in a living Christ before whose tribunal we shall all stand to give account. If Christianity does not have at its base a historically resurrected, ruling, and coming-into-judgment Lord, it is devoid of any power to motivate men to a good life. It would have no "teeth." Morals, in the traditional sense of an absolute standard of right and wrong, cannot exist in the personal economy and providence of one who does not believe in a punitive God. Most of us have figured out that if there is no divine justice beyond the grave, then there is little power to restrict the only lives we have to some otherwise outdated notions about self-denial.

Huxley was right, at least in this respect, that if society is to be morally restrained from going berserk there must be a belief in God who plans to bring every last one of us into judgment before him.

Historic Christianity

When we move through the New Testament back to the Christian faith as defined by those men who originally preached it, it emerges as God's own devised system of redemption from sin and death and certain judgment. For proof, men were pointed toward what they evidently considered to be contemporary facts: the death and resurrection of Jesus Christ. To them, Christianity was eminently more than a moral system since the resurrection proved that Christ was more than a man.

While ancient Oriental cults linked the annual cycle of winter and summer to the death and resurrection of the mythical Adonis, Christianity deals with no such mythology. It offers a real historical founder, plus accounts of his remarkable death, burial, and resurrection in well-written documents which have passed the most severe tests known to us today for historical accuracy and authenticity (which we will elaborate on in the next two chapters). Christianity exists now because of what happened to the historical Jesus. It is not the result of doctrines and principles, but of events in the life of Jesus of Nazareth.

The Nature of Christianity

Apart from this truly historical base, the real Christian religion cannot exist. Its nature is historical and redemptive, not simply moral. Morality is certainly inherent in its nature, but its great thrust is redemption from the death penalty. Its promise is eternal life. No social gospel or moralistic doctrine can make good on promises like that. Only Christ's own sinless life, substitutionary death, and resurrection has power to bring that about. It is essential, therefore, that a truly sinless life, a real death by crucifixion, and a resurrection back to life in his own body be experienced by a genuinely historic Jesus in order to give power to Christianity's claim to a future life without end.

Here is the beginning place for an investigation into the genuineness of Christianity. It must begin with a real, historic, space-time Jesus; for apart from his own historical existence, neither redemption nor resurrection could amount to any more than pie-in-the-sky-by-and-by.

EVIDENCE FOR THE HISTORICAL JESUS

Commenting on the uniqueness of the New Testament's claim for Jesus, Michael Green has observed,

> *It is all about the Jesus of history. Remove him from Christianity and nothing distinctive is left. Once disprove the historicity of Jesus Christ, and Christianity will collapse like a pack of cards. For it all depends on this fundamental conviction, that God was made manifest in human flesh. And that is a matter not of ideology or mythology but history.*[1]

Just how well founded the claim for the historical Jesus is will be seen in the evidence as follows.

1. Michael Green, *Runaway World*, Inter-Varsity Press, p. 12.

From Pagan Sources

Palestine of the first century has been referred to as an unimportant frontier province in the Roman Empire. Those provincial governors assigned to that region of the world were often thought to have received hardship posts. Too, those who wrote the history of Rome were in the upper strata of Roman society and usually had a personal dislike of Orientals, disapproved of their religions and looked upon their superstitions as very un-Roman.[2] This partially accounts for the little trickles of information that comes from their pens about the Christian religion. They wrote about it only as it forced its way into the mainstream of their view. Yet what they did write is proof positive that Jesus Christ was both a real person and that he had made such an impact upon society that the Roman world found it increasingly difficult to disregard him.

1. *Thallus*

Our initial witness makes a contribution of a unique sort inasmuch as he had no intention of making Christianity to appear genuine. To the contrary, Thallus, a Samaritan-born historian who lived and worked in Rome about A.D. 52, wrote to offset the supernatural element which accompanied the crucifixion. Though the writings of

2. Ibid., p. 12.

Thallus are lost to us, Julius Africanus, a Christian chronographer of the late second century, was familiar with them and quotes from them. In a comment on the darkness that fell upon the land during the crucifixion (Mark 15:33), Africanus says that "Thallus, in the third book of his histories, explains away this darkness as an eclipse of the sun."[3] Africanus stated his objection to the report arguing that an eclipse of the sun cannot occur during the full moon, as was the case when Jesus died at Passover time. The force of the reference to Thallus is that the circumstances of Jesus' death were known and discussed in the Imperial City as early as the middle of the first century. The fact of Jesus' crucifixion must have been fairly well known by that time, to the extent that unbelievers like Thallus thought it necessary to explain the matter of the darkness as a natural phenomenon. Will Durant observed that Thallus' "argument took the existence of Christ for granted."[4] Neither Jesus nor the darkness at his death were ever denied as factual. Durant summed up the matter of Christ's historical existence for himself by saying that it never occured to the early opponents of Christianity to deny the existence of Jesus.[5] Ironically, Thallus' efforts have been turned into the mainstream of historical proof for Jesus and for the reliability of Mark's account of the darkness at his death.

3. F. F. Bruce, *The New Testament Documents*, Eerdmens, p. 113.
4. Will Durant, *Caesar and Christ*, Simon and Schuster, p. 555.
5. Ibid.

2. *Mara Bar-Serapion*

F. F. Bruce, Rylands professor at Manchester University, tells of a manuscript in the British Museum preserving the text of a letter sent to his son by a Syrian named Mara Bar-Serapion. In prison at the time of the writing, the father pleads with his son to be wise. He illustrated the folly of persecuting wise men like Socrates, Pythagoras, and the wise king of the Jews, which the context obviously shows to be Jesus.

> *What advantage did the Athenians gain from putting Socrates to death? Famine and plague came upon them as a judgment for their crime. What advantage did the men of Samos gain from burning Pythagoras? In a moment their land was covered with sand. What advantage did the Jews gain from executing their king? It was just after that that their kingdom was abolished. God justly avenged these three wise men: the Athenians died of hunger; the Samians were overwhelmed by the seas; the Jews, ruined and driven from their land, live in complete dispersion. But Socrates did not die for good; he lived on in the teaching of Plato. Pythagoras did not die for good; he lived on in the statue of Hera. Nor did the wise King die for good; he lived on in the teaching which He had given.*[6]

6. British Museum Syriac Mss., F. F. Bruce, *Jesus and Christian Origins Outside the New Testament,* p. 31.

Some inaccuracies exist in the letter, says Bruce, about Samos and Athens, but the references to Christ and to the Jews are undeniably accurate, and there is no denying the historical existence of the three men mentioned. By the time this letter was written, Jesus had already received a place of recognition equal to the sages of the ages. Jesus was as real a person of history as was Socrates and Pythagoras.

3. *Tacitus, Pliny, Suetonius*

Three Roman officials, who held stature with emperors as well as with the empire, wrote of Jesus in such a way as to take his historical existence for granted. Their writings appeared at the turn of the second century.

The first of these, usually rated as the greatest of Roman historians, was Cornelius Tacitus, who was born about A.D. 52-54. At about the age of sixty, while writing of the reign of Nero (A.D. 54-68), he told how the Christians were made scapegoats for the Great Fire of Rome in A.D. 64. It had been rumored that Nero had himself started the fire so that he could attain to glory by rebuilding the great capital city in more glorious fashion. When Tacitus wrote about this, he mentioned Jesus by the name of Christus:

> *Consequently, to get rid of the report, Nero fastened the guilt and inflicted the most exquisite tortures on a class hated for their*

> *abominations, called Christians by the populace. Christus, from whom the name had its origin, suffered the extreme penalty during the reign of Tiberius at the hands of one of our procurators, Pontius Pilatus.*[7]

To Tacitus, a pagan who knew little or nothing of Jewish messianism, "Christus" was more than likely only a proper name; but to him, Christus was as real as the Roman procurator who executed him.

C. Plinius Secundus, called Pliny the Younger to distinguish him from his uncle, the elder Pliny, was governor of Bithynia about A.D. 112. He often wrote to the Emperor Trajan asking his Imperial advice on how best to deal with the problem of the Christians in his province. According to him, they were causing trouble. In one of his letters, he spoke of Christ as he reported of some information which he extracted from some Christian girls by torture, "They were in the habit of meeting on a certain fixed day before it was light, when they sang an anthem to Christ as God, and bound themselves by a solemn oath not to commit any wicked deed . . . after which it was their custom to separate, and then meet again to partake of food, but food of an ordinary kind."[8]

Pliny seemed to be perplexed by the innocence of the whole matter, and perhaps to keep from coun-

7. *The Annals and the Histories*, 15:44. From Britannica Great Books, Vol. 15, p. 168.

8. Epistles, 10:96.

termanding any governmental policies about Christians, he thought it best to write to the Emperor before taking any action.

There is also a testimony to the historical Jesus from Suetonius, annalist and court official of the Imperial House during the reign of Hadrian. About A.D. 120, he wrote the *Life of Claudius*. From this work comes his most famous statement: "As the Jews were making constant disturbances at the instigation of Chrestus, he (Claudius) expelled them from Rome."[9] The reason for the fame of this quotation is due to the fact that Luke, some sixty years earlier, had recorded this same incident as the reason for the apostle Paul yoking up with a Christian Jewish couple named Aquila and Priscilla (Acts 18:1-2). Again, the mention of Christ in the historical context is observed in extra-biblical literature.

After having referred to the above three Roman officials as an evidence for the actual existence of Jesus Christ, Durant explains that while these references prove the existence of Christians rather than of Christ, unless we assume that Christ did indeed live, we will be driven to the "improbable hypothesis that Jesus was invented in one generation; moreover we must suppose that the Christian community in Rome had been established some years before 52, to merit the attention of an imperial decree."[10]

9. *Life of Claudius*, 25:4.
10. Durant, *Caesar and Christ*, p. 555.

When this evidence is compiled in the company of such an historian as Tacitus and with Roman officials of the stature of Pliny and Suetonius, it makes the historical reality of Jesus as certain as that of any outstanding figure of antiquity.

From Jewish Sources

1. *The Talmud*

There are two separate books of writings dealing with Jewish law called the Talmud. The first of these is the Mishnah, which is the Jewish code of religious jurisprudence. It began to be compiled sometime after the destruction of Jerusalem in A.D. 70 and was completed about A.D. 200. This great body of newly codified case law became the object of Jewish study from which grew a body of commentaries called Gemaras. Together, the Mishnah (the law book) and the Gemara (the commentary) are called the Talmud. Being Jewish, suffice it to say, all references to "Yeshu'a of Nazareth" in the Talmudic writings are unfriendly, but nevertheless sufficient in number to establish beyond doubt his historical reality.

2. *Josephus*

The most important references to the historical Jesus from a Jewish source is from a former Jewish general turned historian by the name of Flavius Josephus. In his writings he tells us who he was, what he did, and his own evaluation of a historian.

He wrote of many of the outstanding persons we read of in the New Testament: Pilate; Quirinius of Syria (during whose governorship Rome enrolled the Empire for taxation purposes); the Caesars; the Herods; the Pharisees and the Sadducees; Annas and Caiaphas, who had Jesus crucified; Felix and Festus, under whose governorships the apostle Paul was arrested and before whom he spoke of Jesus; Jesus' brother, James; and John the Baptist.

Most significant is his reference to Jesus himself in the following words:

> *And there arose about this time Jesus, a wise man, if indeed we should call him a man; for he was a doer of marvelous deeds, a teacher of men who receive the truth with pleasure. He won over many Jews and also many Greeks. This man was the Messiah. And when Pilate had condemned him to the cross at the instigation of our own leaders, those who had loved him from the first did not cease. For he appeared to them on the third day alive again, as the prophets had predicted and said many other wonderful things about him. And even now the race of Christians, so named after him, has not yet died out.*[11]

All attempts to discredit this reference to Jesus as having been dressed up by a Christian copiest have failed. The reference is included in all of the

11. Antiquities, 18, 3. 3.

manuscripts of Josephus, including the copy from which the fourth-century historian, Eusebius, read and quoted.

At the close of his excellent book offering evidence for the historical reliability of the New Testament, F. F. Bruce has observed,

> *Whatever else may be thought of the evidence from early Jewish and Gentile writers . . . it does at least establish, for those who refuse the witness of Christian writings, the historical character of Jesus himself. Some writers may toy with the fancy of a 'Christ-myth,' but they do not do so on the ground of historical evidence. The historicity of Christ is as axiomatic for an unbiased historian as the historicity of Julius Caesar. It is not historians who propagate the 'Christ-myth' theories.*[12]

From the New Testament

Whatever reasons may be given for accepting the testimonies of Josephus or of Tacitus or of any other writer from antiquity as reliable histories, to be fair and consistent, must be equally applied to the New Testament writers. Fairness demands that we give at least the same consideration to the New Testament books as we would to any other writing from the same period. All of the New Testament writers were contemporaries of Jesus.

12. F. F. Bruce, *The New Testament Documents*. p. 119.

Five were eyewitnesses, three accompanied Jesus throughout his ministry, and all of their writings are in remarkable agreement. In addition to this, their writings continue to stand the tests of genuineness and historicity. These New Testament writings are by no means the least of the evidence testifying to the actual existence of Jesus as a real person of history. As a matter of fact, if the New Testament books were the only single source from antiquity which presented to us the life of Jesus Christ, that would be more than sufficient proof of his historical reality. It is stated in the *Encyclopaedia Judaica* (Jerusalem) that the fact that Matthew, Mark, Luke, and John have written of Jesus' life is conclusive proof of his reality. That admission from unbelieving Jews should satisfy the most skeptical doubter as to the trustworthiness of the evidence.

H. G. Wells rejected the supernatural element in the gospels, but nevertheless used them as his source material for writing about Jesus and the spread of Christianity in the first century. He admitted that the gospel accounts carried the conviction of reality and felt compelled to say of Jesus, "Here was a man. This part of the tale could not have been invented."[13] Will Durant wrote, "That a few simple men should in one generation have invented so powerful and appealing a personality,

13. H. G. Wells, *The Outline of History,* Vol. I, p. 420.

so lofty an ethic and so inspiring a vision of human brotherhood, would be a miracle far more incredible than any recorded in the Gospels."[14]

The fact of the historical Jesus of Nazareth, as supplied to us by sources both friendly and hostile, is seen to be an indisputable matter. It is conclusive that there was a real Jesus, a man of outstanding character and of unique personality and ability, whose life and teaching truly "constitute the most fascinating feature in the history of Western man."[15] We can be as certain of this fact as we can of any matter of history.

The Practical Value of Knowing That Jesus Lived

He Lived, So What?

With the evidence before us, we can expect most atheists to admit that Jesus lived. But the fact that he existed does not convince us he is God. Practicality leads us to ask if there is any real value to modern men in knowing this single fact?

It Admits to the Reliability of the New Testament

We have all made admissions to one thing or another, while we were unaware that we had admitted to other things at the same time. If, for

14. Will Durant, *Caesar and Christ*, p. 557.
15. Ibid.

example, we say that the Bible is the word of God, we are admitting that there is a God. By the same token, if we admit that Jesus was a great man of history, as most of us certainly do, though we may not be aware of it, we have also admitted that the New Testament is historically reliable. To determine this, consider three things: First, Jesus has received a place of preeminence among the great men of history. Second, men do not receive such recognition merely because they have existed; they must either say or do something that is considered to be truly great. Third, the only source of information from which we can reproduce the great life of Jesus Christ is the New Testament. Beyond the New Testament books, we can know only that he lived and that he was crucified by Pilate in Jerusalem. To know of his works, his personality, his life and teachings, his death and resurrection, in short, what it was that made him great, we are totally dependent on the New Testament. It seems conclusive that a recognition of the greatness of Jesus is, at least to an appreciable degree, an admission of the historical reliability of the New Testament which tells us about him.

This conclusion is of great practical value to those who would know whether the New Testament expresses an outdated sentiment or whether it is actually a historical revelation from God for the redemption of ruined humanity.

2

The Historical Reliability of the New Testament (1)

Mark's record had to survive the acid test of any journalistic or historical writing—being published at a time when it could be read, criticized, and if inauthentic denounced by thousands of Jews, Christians, Romans and Greeks who were living in Palestine at the time of Jesus' ministry.

—Louis Cassels

Historical Accuracy of the Records is Necessary

If it were ever proven that Confucius never lived, Confucianism could still survive. That's because Confucianism rests on what "Confucius say," not on what he did. But apart from history, Christianity could not have begun. That's because it is founded on who Jesus was and what he did while he was here. He was raised from the dead; therein lies the proof of his claim to be the son of God and his power to make good on his claims. The real power of the Christian religion is in the belief that we are going to be redeemed from our coffins in the cemetery. It doesn't take a Solomon to see that Christ's real resurrection is the historical proof of our own resurrection. But to produce belief in an event of that nature requires a sound and solid basis of convincing evidence.

That's where the New Testament comes in: it provides the historical evidence for Christ's life and resurrection. That is the reason why Matthew, Mark, Luke, and John wrote their gospel accounts and the book of Acts, so that people to whom they could not speak personally could have a written testimony of the same things that the eyewitnesses were declaring to have seen and heard. The letters following Acts also contain a great deal of evidence of this kind, though it is usually of an incidental nature.

Since the evidence for Christ is deposited in these books, it is essential to be able to accept their contents as absolutely reliable, not as imaginary. And since belief comes from an honest consideration of the evidence, it becomes essential to demonstrate that the New Testament is a totally reliable account of those historical events that form the basis of that evidence.

People today should realize that they have access to the facts which will enable them to determine for themselves that the New Testament is a reliable record of historical truth. It was never intended for Christian evidences to be confined to the so-called intelligentsia nor that it should be expressed in difficult theological terminology. From the outset, the gospel was preached to the people. The resurrection of Jesus Christ was declared to be a fact, and the evidence was brought to bear upon it. Whether a man could read and write was of no consequence, if he had presence of mind to reason the evidence to a conclusion. Today's people have that same evidence delivered by those first century eyewitnesses, the only difference being that we have their written testimony rather than their bodily presence.

The New Testament is Needed to Reproduce the Life of Christ

Precisely here, at the point of this written testimony, we want to drive a nail of remembrance into the mind, that point being that the New Testament books contain nearly all of the information we presently have about Jesus Christ. While there is an abundance of literature coming down to us from first century Roman, Jewish, and Greek writers, the combined information from all these sources about Jesus amounts to precious little more than the fact that he lived and died at Jerusalem. We are, in fact, totally dependent on the New Testament to reproduce the life and teachings, the personality, and the multitude of events surrounding the death, burial, and resurrection of Jesus.

What That Means to Us Today

What that means in terms of authentic representation of what Jesus actually said and did is this: no theologian, preacher, or historian can say with any authority at all that Jesus said or did anything different from what the New Testament says he did. One may reject the New Testament as a reliable source of information about Christ, but since it is practically the only source we have, then, any statement that he said or did anything to any degree different from the New Testament account of it, is a statement which is purely conjectural and without evidence to sustain it.

Remember, if it is about Jesus Christ, it has to be in the New Testament, or you do not have to believe it—no matter who says it.

The New Testament in the Historical Context

Skeptics often call the Bible a myth. But to read mythology and compare it with the Bible is to know the difference; there is no resemblance at all. Myths are like Peter Pan's never-never land—you cannot locate "once upon a time in a far away place" in either space or time. The New Testament, however, is written in the context of a space-time dimension, providing us with the check points for a confirmation. The historical manner in which the New Testament is written allows verification from other documents of that same period which reflects the accuracy of its statements in regard to the geography, economics, politics, culture, climate, language, morals, and religions of the time. This is the framework of history in which the written testimony to Jesus has been couched.

Archeology

For nearly two centuries, archeology has been unearthing ancient artifacts which continued to corroborate the historical statements of the New Testament.

The "Acid Test"

When we understand that the New Testament has had to pass the "acid test," as one journalist expressed it, we will appreciate far more how firm the foundation for the Christian faith is. Mr. Louis Cassels of United Press International reported in the *Nashville Banner* (April 1, 1972) on the much publicized papyrus discovery by professor Jose O'Callagahan of the Pontifical Biblical Institute at Rome. O'Callagahan's discovery consisted of nineteen tiny papyrus scraps found among the Dead Sea Scrolls and has been identified as fragments from the Gospel of Mark. Excitement centered upon the date of the fragments which was established by scientific methods as having been in a

Palestinian library in A.D. 50. Of course, this indicates that the Gospel of Mark would have already been in circulation only about a dozen years after Jesus' death. What is important to us is Mr. Cassel's observation:

> *This is very important because it means Mark's record had to survive the acid test of any journalistic or historical writing—being published at a time when it could be read, criticized, and if inauthentic denounced by thousands of Jews, Christians, Romans, and Greeks who were living in Palestine at the time of Jesus' ministry. That the early church chose Mark as one of the only four gospels (out of dozens in circulation) to be preserved for posterity in the New Testament also indicates the people closest to the events—Jesus' original followers—found Mark's report accurate and trustworthy, not myth, but true history.*

That is what is meant by the "acid test," and all New Testament books have passed it. This is decisive inasmuch as the New Testament books were not written two or three hundred years after the events happened. They were all written a few years later and were circulated amid the very people among whom the events were reported to have happened while they were still alive to deny them. But rather than deny them, many became Christians and preserved the writings as the genuine accounts of what actually happened.

Unless we can prove that the writers of the New Testament were fakes, we have to accept their testimony for the same reasons we would accept the testimony of Tacitus or Josephus.

The Letters of Paul

Among each new term of freshmen students, we have a momentary bit of confusion because of my placing Paul's letters ahead of the gospels in the Evidences Course Guide for an examination of their historical content and accuracy. Predictably, many of our freshmen think the gospels were written first because they appear first in the New Testament; first the gospels, then Acts, then the letters, then Revelation. This arrangement best fits the sequence of the history of Christianity; first the life of Christ (gospels), then the establishment and spread of the church (Acts), and then the correction and further instruction of Christians (letters). But it was Paul who wrote the first books of the New Testament (unless O'Callagahan's discovery about Mark's gospel is correct). Ten of his letters were written before the traditional date of Mark's gospel, which is A.D. 60-62. The other gospels came later, with John's gospel last.

Let's clear up another bit of misinformation about the letters and their historical content. Following a lecture on this subject in Huntsville, Alabama, a young man asked what kind of verification could be brought to bear on Paul's letters. He explained that it was plain enough to see the historical content of the gospels and Acts, but that that kind of verification could not be made from the letters since, as he thought, "they are doctrine and not history." It only took a moment to point out several instances where Paul's letters abound in historical references which are inextricably bound up with the Christian doctrine. Very often the historical truth of Paul's letters determined the truth of his doctrine.

An example of this phenomenon is the Galatian letter. In the first two chapters, some major events in Paul's life over a period of seventeen years are painstakingly laid out as a solid basis of evidence to back up his claim (which had come under fire) that he was an apostle by direct appointment from the risen Christ, and that he had also received his gospel instruction from Christ. He made his defense by appealing to the Galatians' knowledge of four incidents in his life which were designed to prove to them that the accusations against him were false and his own claims were true. If the Galatians were not familiar with Paul's recollections, as he took for granted they were, his self-defense would have backfired. They would have said that they didn't know what he was talking about and didn't appreciate his trying to bamboozle them into thinking they did. The fact that the Galatian churches preserved the letter as apostolic is proof that they considered all of its historical references as accurate.

Paul told the Corinthian church that over five hundred Christians had seen the Lord alive after his crucifixion and that most of them were still alive at the time as ready references (1 Corinthians 15:6). That letter was written early, yet no one ever tried to gainsay the point, though there were critics from the beginning. Later, in another letter, he reminded them of the miracles he worked in their presence as a proof of his apostleship (2 Corinthians 12:12). How was he able to get away with such a statement if it were not true? The fact that he answered questions from the Corinthians concerning the purposeful use of miracles which he had enabled them to perform takes those miracles for granted (1 Corinthians 12). No effort was ever made by the apostles to prove that they could work miracles. Real miracles do not need proof; they are proof (Mark 16:19-20). In the letters to the Corinthians and the Galatians (3:5), miracles are taken for granted as a part of the facts in the case to which the apostle addressed himself. Keep in mind that the miraculous incidents are recorded in the same matter-of-fact style in which the other historical incidents are recorded. The miracles cannot be extracted from the context of the letters without destroying the continuity of thought and Paul's apostleship which is built upon them.

Paul's references to persons obviously known by his readers shows the true-to-life world in which Christianity was being practiced. (See Romans

16:1-23; 1 Corinthians 1:14-16; 16:17-18; Ephesians 6:21; Philippians 4:2-3; Colossians 1:7; 4:7-17; 1 Timothy 1:20; 2 Timothy 1:5.) He referred to sister churches which were engaged in relief activities for the poor saints in Jerusalem during a famine crisis (Romans 15:25-27; 1 Corinthians 16:1-6). His sketches of intimate friendship with the young evangelist, Timothy, and of his yearning for personal fellowship (Philippians 2:19-20; 2 Timothy 1:2-5; 2:1; 4:4-13) lift the context of Paul's letters out of the realm of literary invention. In addition, his instructions involving the slave culture (Ephesians 6:5-9; Colossians 3:22-4:1), his delineation of the sickening morals which characterized his generation (Romans 1:24-32, which was corroborated by Gentile writers of that period), his warnings against false teachers preying on the churches (2 Corinthians 11), and the fact that his letters were preserved by the churches, all combine to produce a context which has that ring of historical certainty.[16]

Don't Forget the Point

Remember that in this book our method for proving the claims for Christ and for Christianity is the same method used by the apostles and New

16. Satisfaction can be obtained in this matter by reading Sir William Ramsay's, *Paul the Traveler and Roman Citizen*, Baker Book House.

Testament writers. We are going to examine the same evidence which they offered for consideration and then reproduce their own reasoning from that evidence for believing in Christ. We are not fashioning new arguments; there are none. Our purpose in this book is to point modern man back to the only real evidence there is for Christ—the evidence of the eyewitnesses themselves as preserved for us in the New Testament documents. Our purpose is to reproduce their own case for belief. It is to date the most successful case for Christ ever advanced. But the record containing that evidence is going to have to be completely trustworthy; we must have complete confidence that it contains nothing but the truth, if we accept their evidence as real and not manufactured in their own imaginations. The point, then, of these early chapters is to produce sound reasons for trusting those New Testament records to be fully reliable. Then we can weigh the evidence for ourselves and draw our own conclusions about Christ, which is what was intended from the beginning. Since Christianity is an individual relationship to Christ by faith, each individual must make his own judgment in the matter. The purpose of this book is to point you toward the ground of that judgement.

The Gospels and Acts

In the first century, Christianity became a system of life and action with such a momentous impact that it invaded every social stratum of every culture in the Roman Empire. Historians who deal with those forces which they suppose contributed to the shape of civilization must concern themselves with the facts that gave Christianity its power to invade the Roman world, to powerfully touch the people in every social stratum, and to persist through the rigors of persecution and on through the ages to greatly affect our present time. To accomplish this task, the historian must turn to those ancient documents which furnish him the information he needs. Without exception they turn to the gospels and Acts for that information.

Examples from Luke

Consider Luke's opening statement to Theophilus as a contrast between mythology and history. Luke assured Theophilus that the material he wrote had been carefully researched, that it had been secured from the eyewitnesses themselves, that it was written with accuracy, and that the events which were to be recounted were chronologically arranged in the order in which they happened. Then he stated that the purpose of such painstaking detail and precision of writing was that Theophilus, who had already heard something of the gospel, might "know the certainty concerning the things wherein [he] . . . wast instructed" (Luke 1:4). Now that is the language of the historian, not of mythology, not even of historical romance.[17] In what way other than a miracle could Luke or anyone else have confirmed to Theophilus the certainty of the events of Christianity? The only way to certify to others events which they have not seen is to record them in some manner, whether on film or tape or in written form. This allows for their verification. Both Luke and Acts abound in historical references which have been verified by men of exceptional expertise in archaeology and history. Sir William Ramsay's research confirmed Luke's accuracy and historical genius and assigned to him a place among the historians of the highest quality.[18] F. F. Bruce quotes the verdict of the present professor of classics at Auckland University in New Zealand as saying that "Luke is a consummate historian, to be ranked in his own right with the great writers of the Greeks."[19]

Also, Professor Bruce has shown how Luke has set his story in the context of imperial history. Three emperors are mentioned by name: Augustus, Tiberius, and Claudius. The birth of Jesus is fixed

17. Historical romance is a skillful integration of fact and fiction which supplies a continuity of thought by linking real persons and places and events together with a story-telling of the author's own creation. But for all its historical references, it fails to be a documentary at all points, and for obvious reasons does not claim to be. For this reason, the New Testament bears no faint resemblance to historical romance; it claims to be a historically accurate document at every point, and confirmation to date is without exception to that claim.

18. Ramsay, *Paul, Traveler & Roman Citizen*, p. 4.

19. Bruce, *New Testament Documents*, p. 91.

in the reign of Emperor Augustus, when Herod the Great was king of Judaea and when Quirinius was governor of Syria. John the Baptist's public ministry is elaborately dated by a series of synchronisms "in the Greek historical manner," says Bruce, "reminding the classical student of the synchronisms with which, for example, Thucydides dates the formal outbreak of the Pelopenesian War."[20] Outstanding names among both Jews and Gentiles of that day appear in Luke's account—Pilate, Sergius Paulus, Gallio, Felix, Festus, Herod the Great and some of his descendants, Herod Antipas the tetrarch of Galilee, the vassal kings Herod Agrippa I and II, Bernice and Drusilla, and leading members of the Jewish priestly caste such as Annas, Caiphas, and Gamaliel—all of whom are mentioned in other documents outside the New Testament.

The "acid test" was what Bruce had in mind when he wrote, "A writer who thus relates his story to the wider context of world history is courting trouble if he is not careful; he affords his critical readers so many opportunities for testing his accuracy"[21] Bruce continues: "He puts his picture in the framework of contemporary history in a way which would inevitably invite exposure if his work were that of a romancer, but which in fact provides a test and vindication on historical grounds of the trustworthiness of his own writings."[22]

20. Ibid., p. 8.
21. Ibid., p. 82.
22. Ibid., p. 92.

Jesus' Birth

Christ's birth is set squarely in the context of first century Palestine, where it was affected by the decrees of Caesar. Luke records that historic event in the following words:

> *Now it came to pass in those days, there went out a decree from Caesar Augustus, that all the world should be enrolled. This was the first enrolment made when Quirinius was governor of Syria. And all went to enrol themselves, every one to his own city. And Joseph also went up from Galilee, out of the city of Nazareth, into Judaea, to the city of David, which is called Bethlehem, because he was of the house and family of David; to enrol himself with Mary, who was betrothed to him, being great with child. And it came to pass, while they were there, the days were fulfilled that she should be delivered. And she brought forth her firstborn son; and she wrapped him in swaddling clothes, and laid him in a manger, because there was no room for them in the inn.* (Luke 2:1-7)

Just a few years ago, Bible critics believed that Luke had made about as many mistakes as could be made in this short paragraph. It was charged that Luke was in error about the very existence of an imperial decree for the purpose of taxation; it was challenged that Quirinius was even governor of Syria at that time, and it was denied that everyone had to go to his ancestral home to be enrolled for such a purpose. Yet, Joseph P. Free, professor of Bible and Archaeology at Wheaton College, has confirmed, through the recent discoveries of archaeology, the absolute reliability of Luke's report on these very points. Professor Free documents the discovery of a number of papyrus writings which relate to Roman census taking showing that such a census was made every fourteen years, and he cites one made about 9-6 B.C.[23] He tells us of an inscription found at Rome in 1828 indicating that Quirinius was governor of Syria, not once but twice, and also that William Ramsay, just before World War I, had found a monument in Asia Minor likewise implying two governorships for Quirinius. One of these governorships has been established at A.D. 6. Free also says that archaeology has confirmed that the governor of Egypt during the Roman rule made an edict in A.D. 104, showing that at the very time of that census, the people were to return to their ancestral homes for the enrolling. Free states emphatically that, "it is evident that archaeological discoveries testify to the validity of Luke's statements."[24]

Matthew also records the birth of Christ and Herod's outrageous conduct in the slaughter of the innocent babies in his effort to protect his throne,

23. Joseph P. Free, *Archaeology and Bible History*, Scripture Press, p. 285.

24. Ibid., p. 26.

as he thought, from the new messianic king (Matthew 2:1-16). All efforts of criticism to reflect against the trustworthiness of this account have been both conjectural and contrary to the evidence. Matthew's record of this horrible incident by Herod the Great is in character with all we know from ancient sources, especially from Josephus, about his murderous actions to secure his kingdom for himself. "A man who had his own wife and her mother put to death, his brother-in-law forcibly drowned in a swimming pool, and his own sons strangled—such a man would not have even so much as hesitated in giving the order that the children under two years of age in Bethlehem should be slain."[25]

John's Ministry

Not only does Matthew give us the account of John's prophetic message and boldness in preaching to both Herod and the Jews, but even some of the subtilties, such as his diet of locusts and wild honey and his clothing of camel's hair (Matthew 3:4). All the gospel writers locate his ministry from Jerusalem to the region round about the Jordan (Matthew 3:1; Luke 3:3), and from "Aenon near to Salim" to the River Jordan where he baptized multitudes (John 3:23; Matthew 3:5-6; Mark 1:4-5). Even Herod the Great knew John and held a certain distant respect for him (Mark 6:14-20). Such

25. Ibid., p. 289.

widespread activities and fame would have quite a lasting effect upon the residents of Palestine where John preached, especially since they regarded him as the Lord's prophet (Matthew 14:5) who had been slain (beheaded) by Herod (Matthew 14:1-11). It is inconceivable that any one of the four gospels could have been circulated and accepted as reliable reports by so many persons in the Palestinian area if the things concerning John the Baptist were not actually true. Those people still living at the time of the writing would have known better and would have certainly discredited the account. Since John's ministry is mentioned at the outset of each one of the four gospel reports, it could not have been missed.

Luke dates and locates John's ministry with the precision of a historian:

> *In the fifteenth year of the reign of Tiberius Caesar, Pontius Pilate being governor of Judaea, and Herod being tetrarch of Galilee, and his brother Philip tetrarch of the region of Ituraea and Trachonitis, and Lysanias tetrarch of Abilene, in the high priesthood of Annas and Caiaphas, the word of God came unto John the son of Zacharias in the wilderness.* (Luke 3:1-2)

It is quite confirming to know that every political and religious figure named here has also been mentioned in other writings from this same period of time. What half-smart forger would tie his literary tale to so many known persons and places with any serious intent to deceive? It would be futile.

Christ's Ministry

This dynamic life embraced the great masses of the people in Palestine from Galilee to Judaea and can be definitely calculated to have transpired during the Roman occupation of Palestine, which began from 63 B.C., when the Herodian rule in Judaea was replaced by direct Roman administration in A.D. 6. Confirmations from contemporary writers like Josephus, together with the archaeologists' verifications of the accuracy of the geography, the cultures of the lands, the languages, and the religious and political peculiarities of both the Jews and Gentiles are sufficient proof to any honest investigator as to the reliability of the historical background during the life of Christ which is set out in the gospels.

Jesus' Death and the Beginning of Christianity

The last days of Christ on earth have been carefully detailed in the closing chapters of all four of the gospels. The matters of Christ's death, burial, and resurrection, the beginning of the church and the spread of the Christian religion from Jerusalem to Rome in the face of Jewish hierarchial opposition, and events involving Roman governors and imperial decrees as recorded in the book of Acts could not possibly have been invented in a single generation and then successfully passed off as true on the people of that very generation who knew better. That would have been as impossible as for a writer today to fabricate a story of an unsuccessful Japanese attempt to invade California in the early months of World War II, to locate the invasion landing at Long Beach on December 27th of 1941, to invent speeches and events which were supposed to have happened among the residents of the city due to the invasion, and then to have repelled the invasion by some genius of strategy, and attempt to pass the story off as true on those very people while they were still alive to say otherwise! The New Testament writings could have had no better chance of survival than that if their contents were not true.

The New Testament is not a compilation of mythical stories. It was written in the sane and sober appearance of history and it comes up reliable on investigation. The New Testament records the activities of real people and of actual events. Even though the writers did not compose their books for today's critics, the unmistakable language of the historical context makes them so easily available for verification that the writers might well have said, "Here are the facts; check them out for yourselves!"

3

The Historical Reliability of the New Testament (2)

If the New Testament were a collection of secular writings, their authenticity would generally be regarded as beyond all doubt.
—F. F. Bruce

Just how reliable is our New Testament? It has occurred to many of us that we are removed from the original writers of the New Testament by nearly two thousand years. It's only natural to wonder if we are reading just exactly what they wrote. After all, since we have none of the original writings, just copies, can we be confident that those who copied them did not tamper with them?

Comparison of the New Testament With Classical Histories

Due to the manuscript evidence, we are in a better position to answer that question for the New Testament than we are for the great classical histories. The late Sir Frederick Kenyon, who served as director and librarian of the British Museum, has stated:

> *Besides number, the manuscripts of the New Testament differ from those of the classical authors, and this time the difference is clear gain. In no other case is the interval of time between the composition of the book and the date of the earliest extant manuscripts so short as in that of the New Testament. The books of the New Testament were written in the latter part of the first century; the earliest extant manuscripts (trifling scraps excepted) are of the fourth century—say from 250 to 350 years later. . . . This may sound a considerable interval, but it is nothing to that which parts most of the great classical authors from their earliest manuscripts.*[26]

In order to appreciate the enthusiasm with which Professor Kenyon made that statement, we only need to consider a few examples for testing the reliability of the classical histories and then compare the evidence for the New Testament by that same test.

Classical Attestation

Much of our knowledge of the Caesars is dependent upon the writings of the Roman historian Cornelius Tacitus, who wrote about A.D. 100-115.

26. Frederic Kenyon, *Handbook to the Textual Criticism of the New Testament*, (London: Macmillan and Co. 1901) p. 4.

We have no originals from his hand and only half of the thirty books of histories which he wrote have survived the ravages of time in the form of two manuscript copies. One of these manuscripts is from the tenth century and the other from the eleventh century. That means that there are time gaps of 800 to 1000 years from the originals written by Tacitus himself to the only two copies of his work that we presently possess. Now, while that is quite a distance in time removed from the original writings, this kind of manuscript evidence does not cause undue concern among our classical scholars.

About this same quality of manuscript evidence is characteristic of all the classical histories. Consider Julius Caesar's account of his Gallic Wars, which he wrote between 58 and 50 B.C. While there are several good manuscript copies, the oldest is about 900 years removed from Caesar. Quite a gap! Then, there are two historians from deep antiquity, Thucydides and Herodotus, who wrote during the fifth century before Christ. Of the eight manuscript copies from Thucydides, the earliest is about A.D. 900. That leaves a gap of some 1300 years from the original history to our best copy! And the manuscript attestation for Herodotus is said to be about the same. Yet there is not a classical scholar who would yield a single manuscript copy simply because they are removed by such a gap of time from the originals.

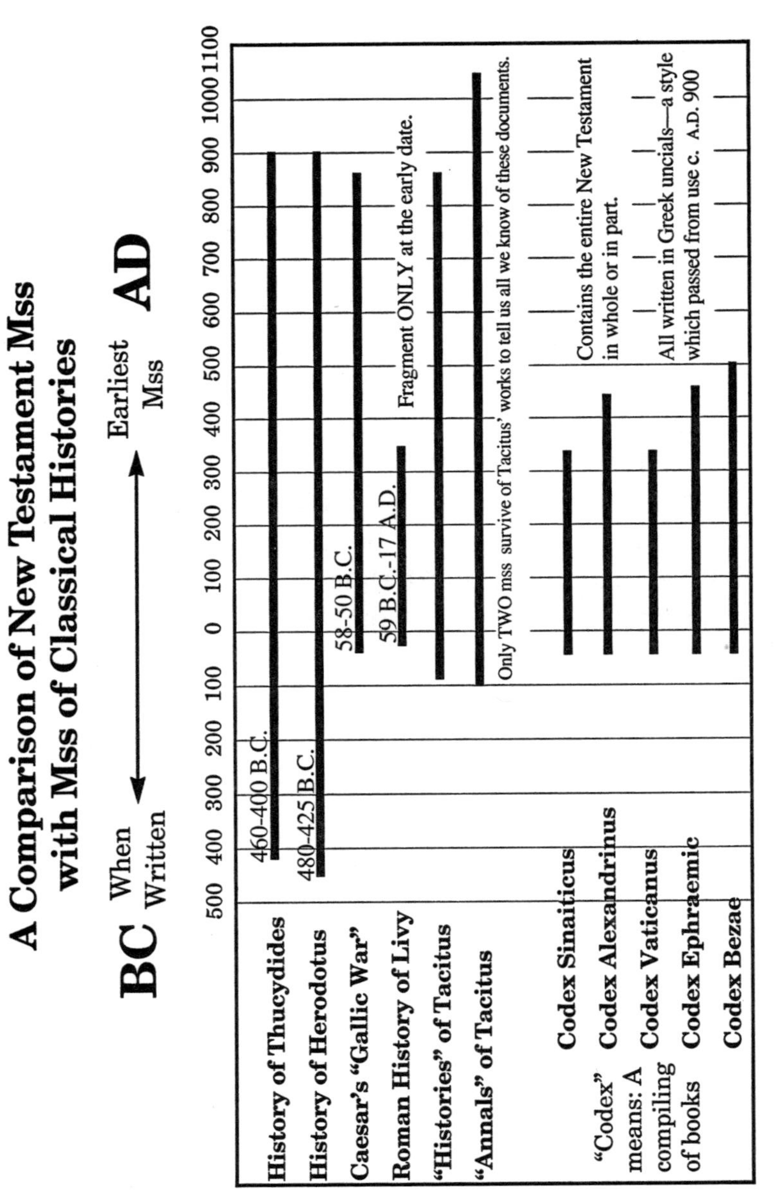
A Comparison of New Testament Mss
with Mss of Classical Histories
BC When Written
Earliest Mss AD
500 400 300 200 100 0 100 200 300 400 500 600 700 800 900 1000 1100
History of Thucydides
460-400 B.C.
History of Herodotus
480-425 B.C.
Caesar's "Gallic War"
58-50 B.C.
Roman History of Livy
59 B.C.-17 A.D.
Fragment ONLY at the early date.
"Histories" of Tacitus
"Annals" of Tacitus
Only TWO mss survive of Tacitus' works to tell us all we know of these documents.
"Codex" means: A compiling of books
Codex Sinaiticus
Codex Alexandrinus
Codex Vaticanus
Codex Ephraemic
Codex Bezae
Contains the entire New Testament in whole or in part.
All written in Greek uncials—a style which passed from use c. A.D. 900

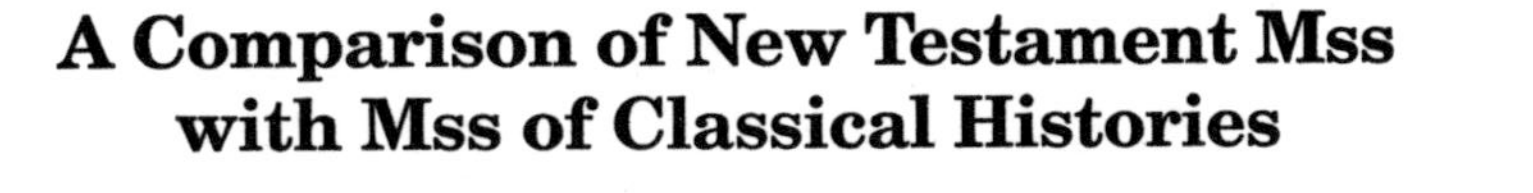

New Testament Attestation

A striking contrast exists between the abundance of New Testament manuscripts and the comparative poverty of the classical copies. There are right now some four thousand copies of the Greek New Testament. Some of these are very ancient, two of them dating back to A.D. 350, leaving a time gap of only 250 years from the original writers to our copies. These two oldest and best copies (each in a book form called a codex) are the Codex Sinaiticus (so called since it was found in 1844 in the monastery of St. Catherine at the foot of Mt. Sinai by the German Bible scholar Constantine Tischendorf) and the Codex Vaticanus (so named because it is kept in the Vatican in Rome). This evidence alone is superior to that for Tacitus' writings. Then there is the Codex Alexandrinus, which is displayed along with the Sinaiticus in the British Museum, and the Codex Bezae from the fifth or sixth century, now located at Cambridge University. And in addition to these, there are hundreds more copies of the quality of the classical manuscripts.

Inasmuch as the classical writings are received as authentic histories on a manuscript basis, which is not nearly as qualitative as that for the New Testament, then how much more should we be confident of the authentic nature of the New Testament. Professor Bruce makes an observation from this basis, apparently with tongue-in-cheek, that "If the New Testament were a collection of secular writings, their authenticity would generally be regarded as beyond all doubt."[27] Also, the Jewish scholar, J. Klausner, said, "If we had ancient sources like those in the Gospels for the history of Alexander or Caesar, we should not cast any doubt upon them whatsoever."[28]

Evidence From the Second Century

Besides the codices, there is still more evidence for the New Testament's reliability from yet another source of an earlier date.

From the Apostolic Fathers

There is a collection of writings nearly as old as the New Testament itself, having come down to us through the efforts of copyists, originally dating from about A.D. 90-160. This collection, written by early Christians, contains quotations from the New Testament in such quantity as to very nearly reproduce it. It is referred to as the writings of the apostolic fathers. This is an unofficial designation attributed to these particular writers since they either had a personal acquaintance with one or more of the apostles or sat at the feet of those who did. Their quotations from the New Testament, then, were very close in time to the original documents. The writings have been translated and pub-

27. Bruce, *New Testament Documents*, p. 15.
28. Will Durant quoting Klausner, *Caesar and Christ*, p. 557.

lished and are readily available in libraries and book stores.

Their Value to Us Today

These writings reveal to us how confident those early Christians were that the New Testament contained nothing but the truth, and that it contained an authentic account of the life and teachings of Jesus. At the close of the first century and during the first part of the second, there were thousands of Christians who put their lives on the line for their faith in the Christ of the New Testament. To them, it was not a matter of conjecture whether the New Testament reported the truth; it was the testimony of history not too far removed from the actual events it described, and some of them, still alive at the end of the first century, had even participated in some of those history-making episodes. Some of them still living in the early second century could tell what the apostles themselves had said, as in the case of Ignatius (70-110) and Polycarp (70-156), who knew the apostles. To them, there was no gainsaying the truth of the New Testament. And for that conviction, most of them suffered hardship and some paid the supreme price.

It is also clear from these early documents that Bible readings from the New Testament became a regular part of the Christian life in the second century. Both Clement of Alexandria (who died about 220) and Tertullian (who died about 230) agreed that married people should read the Scriptures together before the chief meal of the day.[29] From another epistle (falsely attributed to Clement) we learn of cottage meetings where wealthy Christians had purchased Bibles for reading the Scriptures aloud.[30] Origen (about 185-254) recalled daily Bible readings and Scripture recitations as a child.[31] And Irenaeus (about 120-202) encouraged Christians to be nourished from the Scriptures.[32]

From Heretics

Even heretics furnish proof that the New Testament had been long written by A.D. 150, and had already attained a place of authority in the church. The writings of the heretical school of Gnosticism headed up by Valentinus (about 130-150) quotes extensively from the New Testament.[33] And a list of several New Testament books which he considered acceptable were drawn up by the heretic, Marcion, about the year 140,[34] furnishing more proof that the New Testament was in circulation by this time.

29. Adolph Harnack, *Bible Reading in the Early Church*, London, 1912, p.55.
30. Ibid., p. 63.
31. H. G. Herklots, *How Our Bible Came to Us*, Oxford University Press, 1957, p. 95.
32. Harnack, *Bible Reading in the Early Church*, p. 53.
33. Bruce, *New Testament Documents*, p. 19.
34. Ibid., p.63.

From a Recently Discovered Fragment

In the John Rylands Library in Manchester, England, there are collections of papyrus fragments which have been catalogued. Among them is one of the most outstanding biblical discoveries of this century. In 1934, Mr. C. H. Roberts, a papyrology student at Oxford, was sorting a group of papyri, which had been acquired from Egypt in 1920, and found a small papyrus scrap quoting John 18:31-33 on one side and verses 37-38 on the other side. This papyrus fragment was dated by the highly-sophisticated method of paleography (determining dates and origins by the style of writing) at about A.D. 125! That is easily the oldest fragment of a copy of the New Testament in our possession. Of course, the original document, or a copy of it, from which this fragment was made, came first. This shoves the original writing back into the first century into the hands of the apostle John, and forever refutes liberalism's accusation that the Gospel of John was not written until the second century.

Such an accumulation of evidence (and we have barely called attention to the great mass of material evidence) is more than sufficient to confirm that the New Testament, just as we have it now, is a near-perfect reproduction of the original apostolic writings. This is the quality of evidence which led Professor Kenyon to announce:

> *The interval then between the dates of original composition and the earliest extant evidence becomes so small as to be in fact negligible, and the last foundation for any doubt that the Scriptures have come down to us substantially as they were written has now been removed. Both the authenticity and the general integrity of the books of the New Testament may be regarded as finally established.*[35]

There is just no book from the past which has been given such a thoroughgoing testimony to its total reliability. And remember that this reliability embraces the two areas that people want to know about most: that the New Testament, as we have it now, is exactly what was originally written by the apostles and that its statements are historically reliable.

A Great Historian's Recommendation

The testimony of Sir William Ramsay is very applicable just here. During the greater part of his life, Sir William was professor of Humanity at the University of Aberdeen in Scotland. He became acknowledged as a historian and an outstanding authority on the life of Paul and of the history of the early church, and he carried on extensive archaeological research in Asiatic Turkey and the Bible lands. His defense of the historical Jesus as

35. Frederic Kenyon, *The Bible and Archaeology*, Harper and Row, 1940, p. 288.

the son of God is particularly convincing when we consider that Ramsay did not begin researching with the same conviction that he later acquired through his research. Ramsay's archaeological studies drove him to have confidence in the New Testament. W. Ward Gasque, in an excellent little biography of this truly great scholar, stated: "It is of great significance that Sir William Ramsay came to the study of the New Testament as a Roman historian rather than as a theologian."[36] Indeed, this was significant inasmuch as Ramsay had earlier held the liberal view of the modernistic Tubigen school that the book of Acts was a second-century production. But his archaeological findings convinced him of the total reliability of that book. He wrote of the matter in the following way:

> *I may fairly claim to have entered on this investigation without any prejudice in favor of the conclusion which I shall now attempt to justify to the reader. On the contrary, I began with a mind unfavorable to it, for the ingenuity and apparent completeness of the Tubigen theory had at one time convinced me. It did not lie in my line of life to investigate the subject minutely; but more recently I found myself often brought in contact with the book of Acts as an authority for the topography, antiquities, and society of Asia Minor.*

36. Sir William Ramsay, *Archaeologist and New Testament Scholar*, p. 28.

> *It was gradually borne in upon me that in various details the narrative showed marvelous truth.*[37]

In another book, Ramsay said that "Luke's history is unsurpassed in respect of its trustworthiness."[38] In still another book reporting New Testament reliability resulting from his archaeological research, he wrote, "Luke is a historian of the first rank; not merely are his statements of fact trustworthy; he is possessed of the true historic sense . . . this author should be placed along with the very greatest of historians."[39]

Ramsay's faith spread to the whole of the New Testament due to the overwhelming evidence which he found in its behalf.

Conclusion

How can we know that Jesus is the son of God? We might ask how we can know of anything which we have not seen? The answer is *testimony*. Someone told us in either words or works left behind. Do we accept as true the outstanding exploits of Alexander the Great and of Julius Caesar? Of course. But why? The answer is always the same—history. But when we refer to history are we not referring to the testimony left by yet

37. Ramsey, *Paul the Traveler and Roman Citizen*, pp. 7, 8.
38. Ramsay, *Luke the Physician*, p. 177.
39. Ramsay, *The Bearing of Recent Discovery on the Trustworthiness of the New Testament*, p. 222.

others? Who doubts that Wellington defeated Napoleon at Waterloo? That Columbus sailed to the Americas in the fifteenth century? That Luther nailed his ninety-five theses to the door of the Wittenberg church in 1517? There is no good reason for doubting these men and these events. The testimony in our possession is absolutely convincing. By the same token, we cannot reject the superlative testimony of the New Testament on any grounds of historical evidence. By the very same methods used to attest the reliability of other ancient writings, the New Testament is confirmed to be every bit as reliable as the classical histories.

The case for belief in Christ as our Saviour-God is the written testimony of the New Testament writers. It is a mistake to think that these men merely asserted that Jesus is the son of God without proof. They have pointed us to the weight of the historical evidence. They have appealed to our intelligence and our ability to weigh the evidence and deduct a logical conclusion and, without fear of contradiction, have offered their testimony in the verifiable context of a space-time dimension. They have only requested that we examine their testimony and honestly weigh the evidence as they have presented it. It then becomes ours to make a decision on the basis of that evidence.

4

Implications of the Resurrection

If Christ hath not been raised, then is our preaching vain, your faith also is vain. Yea, and we are found false witnesses of God.
—Paul

During the course of a discussion on the resurrection, I was once asked, "Why do you place so much emphasis on the resurrection? Can't we just get on with Christianity?" That expressed a present concept of Christianity which has no connection to the historic events of the death and resurrection of Jesus. It equates Christianity with a moral code affecting man's relationship with man, but not touching man's relationship to God. It has absolutely nothing to do with faith in Christ. In effect, that means that the historic Jesus has nothing to do with modern Christianity. This concept not only misses the implications of the resurrection, but completely bypasses the implications upon the Christian faith itself if the resurrection did not in fact take place in space and time.

What the Resurrection Implies

The bodily resurrection of Jesus should obviously imply his godhood (Rom. 1:4). This in turn guarantees his total integrity and his consequent ability to make good on all his claims. Since the resurrection centralizes our trust in Jesus to be totally trustworthy to keep all his promises, then it becomes the ground of our hope for victory over the grave and for incorruptible immortality (John 11:25; 1 Peter 1:3-4). It means that the Old Testament Scriptures are absolutely reliable accounts of the history they report, inasmuch as Jesus himself endorsed them as such. He referred to Jonah's experience in the belly of the fish as a historical prefiguring of his own experience for three days and nights in the tomb and so endorsed the historical reliability of the prophecy of Jonah (Matthew 12:38-41). He spoke of Noah as a real person of history, of the Ark as a real sea-going vessel, and of a worldwide flood which "took them all away" (Matt. 24:37-39). When asked whether it was lawful for a man to put away his wife for every cause, he answered from his historical view of the first two chapters of Genesis that the home is based on God's moral law and that therefore "from the beginning" marriage was intended to be a lasting relationship (Matthew 19:3-9).

In essence, the resurrection implies that Jesus is the son of God and that the Bible is the word of God. It is conclusive that the genuineness of Christianity and the Bible's claim to inspiration stand or fall on the historical reality of the resurrection of Jesus Christ.

No Operating Power Without the Resurrection

The resurrection is the motivating power back of the Christian faith. We could no more expect to get on with Christianity without a belief in the resurrection than we could expect a jet airliner to fly without fuel, for in neither case would there by any operating power. It's the same with Christianity: modern men and women must accept God's terms of obedience of faith in Christ and a radical change of life from the inside out if they want eternal life. But if there is no eternal life after death, what sufficient power is there to motivate willful human beings to order their lives after the example of a dead Nazarene Jew? Only the real resurrection of Christ, as a guarantee of our own future resurrection, can induce a power-motive sufficient to accept his conditions in the face of opposition and persecution, and to maintain that life day by day, faithfully, to the death. Historic Christianity with its conditional requirements cannot be expected to exist, due to the very nature of humanity, without the spirit-impacting motivating power of the resurrection faith.

Those who have chosen a resurrectionless Christianity are being cheated by a religion (if you can call it that) that is powerless to justify from sin, powerless to lift the quality of life above the present human characteristic of immorality, and powerless to give hope and encouragement when injustices are perpetrated upon the innocent to their deaths. Christianity without a resurrection is powerless to give any meaning at all to those faceless millions who are assigned, by no choice of their own, to the misery of hunger and bewilderment which presently characterizes the plight of so many human beings in underdeveloped nations and those pitiful members of humanity in slave-labor camps within the stranglehold of godless economies.

Call it what you will, but if it does not identify with the resurrection-empowered faith as defined in the New Testament, it is not Christianity. Christianity without a resurrection is a farce without a force.

If Christ Hath Not Been Raised

In the book of First Corinthians, the apostle Paul viewed Christianity from the vantage points of the implications upon it if Christ were not raised from the dead. He said,

> *If Christ hath not been raised, then is our preaching vain, your faith also is vain. Yea, and we (the apostles) are found false witnesses of God; because we witnessed of God that*

> *he raised up Christ: whom he raised not up, if so be that the dead are not raised. For if the dead are not raised, neither hath Christ been raised: and if Christ hath not been raised, your faith is vain; ye are yet in your sins. Then they also that are fallen asleep in Christ have perished. If we have only hoped in Christ in this life, we are of all men most pitiable.* (1 Corinthians 15:14-19)

Now that's about as honest as a man can be about his own position, especially when it's under fire. But Paul was a practical man, not a sentimentalist. He was convinced that Christianity was genuine on the basis of the Lord's resurrection. And he was just as convinced that without that one single event it was absolutely worthless. So he candidly laid out the whole matter of the value of the Christian religion, apart from a resurrection, from six points of view. He objectively lays it down that if Christ were not raised, then gospel preaching is vain, faith is vain, the apostles are false witnesses, we are still in our sins, believers have perished at death, and, therefore, Christians are of all men to be pitied the most. Consider why:

1. Gospel preaching is vain.

What would there be to preach without the resurrection? "Gospel" means good news, but good news about justification from sin and salvation from the death penalty would be meaningless without the resurrection. All that hocus-pocus about our coming back from the grave would be as vain as Houdini's boast to return from the dead. Christianity without a resurrection would be like a book without words.

2. Faith is vain.

It is impractical to conceive of the Christian faith apart from a personal faith in the resurrection of Jesus since the object of our belief in eternal life is the Lord Jesus himself. Without his resurrection there would be no one to look to to perform the resurrection. Belief would be useless, even senseless. A so-called leap of faith would be irrational without Christ's resurrection, for who else has ever demonstrated his power to raise the dead and promised to raise us, too?

3. The apostles are false witnesses.

If the stories they told of Christ and his resurrection were not true, it would be ludicrous to regard them as sincere and honest men. From the outset, the apostles convinced thousands of people of the resurrection and consequently of the genuineness of their gospel. Among their evidences was their own personal eyewitness testimonies that they saw Jesus alive after the crucifixion (Acts 2:32; 3:15; 4:19-20; 5:30-32; 10:39-41; 13:30-31; 1 Corinthians 9:1; 15:3-8; 1 John 1:1-3). They said that they ate with him, talked with him, and handled him to see the marks of his crucifixion. But how could they be telling the truth if there was no resurrection of that same Jesus who was crucified? It would be a case, pure and simple, of lying. They would be false witnesses.

4. We are still in our sins.

Again, we are drawn back to the very purpose of Christianity—redemption from sin. Salvation from sin and death is inextricably related to the Lord's death and resurrection. Jesus taught that by his cross he would draw all men to him (John 12:32-33), and Paul taught that the word of the cross had the power to save all men (1 Corinthians 1:18). Why? Because at the cross, Christ became our sin offering by paying the price of our sin and delivering us from its death penalty (Isaiah 53:5-11; Matthew 20:28; 2 Corinthians 5:21; Hebrews 9:26-27; 2:14-15). Then he was raised from the dead, thus proving his deity and redemptive work on the cross. The first gospel sermon was calculated to produce belief in the resurrection of Jesus and, consequently, to put trust in him to provide remission of sins (Acts 2:22-39). Inasmuch as redemption from sin is certified by the resurrection, then without it there can be no redemption. This would mean that Christians are yet in their sins and, like it or not, Christianity would have no salvation to offer of any kind.

5. Believers have perished at death.

That is the only logical conclusion apart from the resurrection. Like the dog, Rover, when he's dead, it's over. Death would be our destiny, nothing more.

6. Therefore, Christians are of all men most pitiable.

How Christians in Paul's day could appreciate that statement. Persecuted, discriminated against, looked upon as fools by a world of unbelievers, and all for nothing! Denying themselves the only lives they would ever have. And for what! If Christ was not raised, they gave themselves for a meaningless sentiment, a false hope perpetrated by false witnesses. What a pity.

Of tremendous consequence is the resulting impact which life without resurrection must essentially have upon present humanity. I say *essentially* because we are threatened with war, poverty, famine, disease, injustice, certain death, and, if no resurrection, then oblivion. Therefore, without this belief, it turns upon human nature to survive in the best possible way. Life's essential goal would be the selfish philosophy to "get yours while you can." That is the very reason why nations built upon godless philosophies and why unbelieving individuals are presently engaged in attaining their desires with an unfeeling disregard for those who get in the way.

Paul knew this and commented that life without belief in the resurrection would lead to a fleshly emphasis on the present and a personal disregard for tomorrow. He philosophized that "If the dead are not raised, let us eat and drink, for tomorrow we die" (1 Corinthians 15:32). In other words, live it up now and hang tomorrow! What logic has the power to contradict that philosophy if there is no resurrection to a tribunal of justice and a sentencing to an eternal penalty?

The implications of the bodily resurrection of Jesus Christ are such that everything New Testament Christianity promises and stands for totally collapses without it. The Christian's trust in Christ and consequent hope for eternal victory over corruption and death could not be generated in our hearts without belief in the resurrection. My own motivation for writing this book is to challenge men and women to determine for themselves whether or not Christ was raised. This can be done only by exercising the powers of reason. Reason's function is to sit in judgment on the evidence and draw an honest conclusion from it. That evidence is of an historical nature; it is completely reliable and requires only a fair amount of reason's effort.

Let us now proceed to the evidence.

5

Evidence From the Burial Tomb

The Resurrection of Jesus Christ (1)

Come, see the place where the Lord lay. And go quickly, and tell his disciples, He is risen from the dead.

—Matthew

Sometime before A.D. 60-62, the traditional date for the writing of Mark, the first gospel, many took it upon themselves to write narratives of the life of Christ, which we can intimate from Luke's opening remarks, contained some greater or lesser degree of reliability (Luke 1:1-4). Luke, having researched the matter from the apostles themselves, was stirred to write his own account of the historical Christ with such space-time precision that he fully guaranteed to his Roman correspondent, Theophilus, that what he had only heard about

Christ to that time was nevertheless true and verifiable. The apostles Matthew and John also contributed their eyewitness accounts and soon these four gospels were accepted by the church as accurate representations of the life of Christ Jesus.

The Evidence Is Factual, Not Fictional

In these four historical narratives, we find the evidence for the resurrection which centers upon the burial tomb. The fact that thousands, who had participated in the events described in these books, were still alive and had become believers and had received the gospels is excellent testimony to their factuality. They have been verified by the same testing methods used to verify the classical histories. Our appeal to them for the real facts in the case is at least as reliable as an appeal to any Greek, Roman, or Jewish writing from that same period. It is not reason's function to determine whether the claim is believable or not before the evidence has come in. When the evidence is trustworthy, it is not difficult to reach a believing conclusion even though it embraces a line of reasoning which extends to the supernatural. No truly objective statement of finality can be honestly pronounced on the reality of the resurrection until the evidence which has been made available to us has been considered. Remember that both archaeology and first century contemporary documents have reflected on the statements in the gospels and have corroborated their historical accuracy so that when we turn to them for the resurrection evidence, we are turning to facts, not to fiction.

John's Evidence

I have chosen to follow the line of reasoning in John 20:1-8 because his evidence makes no appeal to any miraculous event which might be construed as an assumption that the supernatural had happened before it was proven. Even critics and unbelieving historians have admitted this evidence as factual. While we will coordinate the evidence with information from the other gospels, we will base the investigation on John's account.

> *Now on the first day of the week cometh Mary Magdalene early, while it was yet dark, unto the tomb, and seeth the stone taken away from the tomb. She runneth therefore, and cometh to Simon Peter, and to the other disciple whom Jesus loved, and saith unto them, They have taken away the Lord out of the tomb, and we know not where they have laid him. Peter therefore went forth, and the other disciple, and they went toward the tomb. And they ran both together: and the other disciple outran Peter, and came first to the tomb; and stooping and looking in, he seeth the linen cloths lying; yet entered he not in. Simon Peter therefore also cometh, following him, and entered into the tomb; and he beholdeth the linen cloths lying, and the nap-*

> *kin, that was upon his head, not lying with the linen cloths, but rolled up in a place by itself. Then entered in therefore the other disciple also, who came first to the tomb, and he saw, and believed.*

An Objective Testimony

John was totally objective in reproducing the resurrection evidence. He presented his material without any comment as to the implications which might arise from it. He only says that the disciple who came first to the tomb saw and believed—a statement of fact. But his own belief that Jesus was raised was stated at precisely that point in order to draw our attention to the reason for that belief which he had reached on the basis of the facts. He wanted us to know what it was that he saw and, therefore, why he believed. John's effort was designed to prod our powers of reason to draw a conclusion from the evidence.

Four Facts

The facts as we have them are four in number: (1) the stone had been rolled back and the tomb was standing open, (2) the body of Jesus was gone, (3) the grave cloths in which Jesus was buried were still lying in the tomb, and (4) it was Sunday, the first day of the week—a significant fact we will look at. This sequence will provide the line of study by which we will consider the evidence, combining the first two facts (the tomb was both empty and open) into a single unit in order to avoid repetition.

THE OPEN AND EMPTY TOMB

Who Got the Body?

On the third day, Christ's crucified body was gone. The tomb was empty. Removal of Christ's body was necessarily either a human act or an act of God. Either Christ was raised as is claimed, or his body was removed by some sort of human ingenuity. If we can satisfy a line of inquiry which can eliminate the human element as the cause for emptying the tomb, we are left with the conclusion that the supernatural element was present in the removal, and the resurrection will be sustained.

The question to be answered is: Who would, or even could, have taken away the dead body of Jesus? Was it his disciples or his enemies who had him crucified? Either it was one of these, or he was raised from the dead. There is no evidence for another explanation.

Was It the Disciples?

This is precisely the question which the evidence answers. While it has actually been suggested that the disciples themselves, at some undisclosed time, somehow stole past the guards to spirit away the body of Christ, Matthew tells us that sufficient steps were taken to prevent that very thing from happening. He informs us that the chief priests and Pharisees went to Pilate telling him of Christ's prophecy to rise on the third day after the crucifixion. Their concern was to keep the body in the tomb until the third day against any attempt to steal the body and make it appear as if he had been raised. Pilate was sufficiently impressed with their concern that he gave them a Roman guard and permission to seal the tomb (Matthew 27:62-66). A Roman guard posted at the tomb would discourage any attempt to rob it of its contents.[40]

It soon became common knowledge that the Jews had bribed the Roman guard to lie about the matter, saying that the disciples had stolen the body while they slept (Matthew 28 11:15). Such an explanation, however, is inadequate, since sleeping men do not know what is happening around them.

Could anyone have seriously accepted this explanation? It's doubtful. Who could believe that the guards were all sleeping at once, or that at least one of them would not have been awakened by several men rolling back the stone, seeing that "it was exceeding great" (Mark 16:4)? Who could believe

40. Jewish guards would not have placed Caesar's seal upon the tomb. Nor would it have been necessary for the Sanhedrin to have bribed their own soldiers to lie about the incident. In addition, only a Roman guard would have feared that the matter would come to Pilate's ears. Dereliction of duty by Jewish guards would have been of no consequence to Pilate. The large sum of money, therefore, was given to Roman guards with an assurance from the Sanhedrin that if the matter came before the governor they would rid the soldiers of any reason to worry (Matthew 28:11-15).

that not one of the guards was awakened during the time it took to roll back the stone, unwrap the corpse, and then rewrap the burial cloths to make it appear that they had not been tampered with? Who could believe it? It would be easier to believe the resurrection. Any suggestion that the disciples removed the body of Christ is mere speculation without evidence and contrary to existing evidence.

Was It the Jews?

Another speculative theory suggests that the Jews themselves took the body of Christ out of the tomb and put it in another place to keep the disciples from reverencing the tomb. But that action would have been completely contrary to their own statement of purpose to keep the body of Christ in the tomb until the third day after the crucifixion. It would have been a definite advantage to the Jewish position to keep the body entombed until the third day for several reasons. First, Jesus' claim to rise on the third day after his death was common knowledge by the time of the crucifixion (Matthew 27:63), and so it occurred to the Jews that if the disciples stole the body, it would appear as if Jesus had made good his claim. In view of this, their intent was to secure the body under the protection of the Roman guard until the third day. At that time, they could have gone to the tomb and, in the presence of all the disciples, rolled back the stone to expose the corpse and demonstrate conclusively that Jesus had failed to rise from the dead. With that action, Christianity would have been stopped dead, then and there. It's not reasonable to accuse the Jews of emptying the tomb; that puts them at cross-purposes with their stated intentions and their efforts to carry them out.

Another point is that in seven short weeks, Jerusalem was seething with the story of the resurrection. The chief priests were upset because their own Messiah's blood was being brought upon them by the apostles, and they were prepared to go to any lengths to stop it. Well then, if the body had been moved by their order, when the apostles started preaching the resurrection, why didn't they issue an official denial? Why didn't they say, "That's nonsense. The body was moved at our own order"? If that would not have convinced them, then why didn't they call as witnesses those who had carried the body away? If that would not do, then why didn't they tell the people where they had laid the body? That would have exposed the preaching of the apostles as a great lie. Why didn't they do it? Because they had nothing to do with relocating the body, and they could not produce it.

One more valid point about the Jews taking away the body is that all the references to the empty tomb are in the gospels; none come in Acts during the apostles' ministry. Why? Because everyone knew that the tomb was empty and the only question worth discussing was why it was empty and what that proved.

On the outside chance that someone would suggest that a grave robber took away the body, it must be remembered that the same guards would have posed as much a problem for robbers as for anyone else. Besides, graves were robbed for their valuables, not for dead bodies. In this particular case, the only thing of value were the spices which were left behind when Jesus vacated the premises (John 19:39-40).

When the facts are considered, the speculative "possibilities" must be assigned to their place as myths.

Who opened and emptied the tomb of Christ? On the basis of the evidence, it is reasonable to conclude that the disciples could not have done it and that the Jews certainly would not have done it. It is a logical implication from the facts given to us in the gospels that Jesus was raised from the dead. That is as reasonable and intelligent a conclusion as intelligent reasoning can draw from the facts.

The Grave Cloths

One of the most interesting aspects of the evidence for the resurrection is the grave cloths in which Jesus was prepared for burial. This is interesting not only because of their contribution to the evidence but because they are seldom mentioned by unbelievers who readily admit the historical factuality of the empty tomb.

Their Position

John tells us that the grave cloths were left lying in the place where Jesus had been laid to rest. This indicates that Jesus passed through them without disturbing their position. They were lying in the same folded position which formed the outline of the body of Jesus when he had been "wound" in them for burial (Mark 15:46). The burial garments were not disheveled; the tomb was not a strewn mess. Carefully observe what John says and what he does not say. He did not say merely that he and Peter saw the linen cloths. He said they both saw them "lying." Of course, they wouldn't have seen them standing. It would have been enough merely to say, "they entered into the tomb and beholdeth the linen cloths." Why, then, did he say they saw them "lying," unless he was indicating their peculiar position? It seems John is stressing the impact that the position of the grave cloths had on both Peter and John, and he wants to make that impression on his readers. Both Matthew and Mark relate that the women who went early to the tomb were invited to observe the place where the Lord had lain (Matt. 28:6; Mark 16:6). If Jesus was not there, and he wasn't, what would they observe if not the grave cloths. The picture which initially met the eyes of the witnesses was telling. The grave cloths were found lying just as they had been originally folded around the body of Christ. Whether they were lying flat or the sticky spices, acting as a bonding agent, held them in a slightly collapsed cocoon shape, the grave cloths were nevertheless still there in their folds and pressing the mind for answers.

Jewish Burial Customs

The manner in which the Jews dressed their dead for burial is described in the resurrection of Lazarus. After Jesus had commanded the resurrection of Lazarus, John testified, "He that was dead came forth, bound hand and foot with graveclothes; and his face was bound about with a napkin. Jesus saith unto them, Loose him, and let him go" (John 11:44). Though Lazarus was alive again, he was still bound hand and foot with grave clothing and needed some assistance to get out of them. The point is that Jesus was prepared for burial in this same way. He was bound up in a grave cloth with aromatic spices poured into the folds and a face napkin wrapped around his head (John 19:39-40). When Jesus was placed in the tomb, he had been wrapped from head to toe. Now, if Jesus were not raised from the dead, who was it that silently rolled back the stone without the guards knowing it, unwrapped the body of Jesus, then rewrapped the grave cloths with such skill that eyewitnesses could not catch the deception, and finally carried away the body—all without being detected? If you can believe that, you can believe the resurrection.

The Swoon Theory?

The so-called swoon theory contends that Jesus did not actually die, but that he only swooned on the cross and in the cool of the tomb revived. But that is contrary to the fact that all the gospels testify to the death of Jesus while yet on the cross (Matthew 27:50; Mark 15:37; Luke 23:46; John 19:30, 33). Mark even records Pilate's surprise that Jesus was already dead after only a few hours on the cross, but was satisfied when he learned from the centurion in charge of the execution that Jesus was dead (Mark 15:44-45). The swoon theory also fails to answer some pretty tough questions. How did Jesus manage to release himself from the grave cloths? That would be a tough challenge for any man, but more especially for one who had been battered and severely torn by scourging and crucifixion and deeply wounded by the soldier's spear, thrust upwards into his side, making a wound large enough to spill out his lifeblood onto the ground (John 19:34). And how, after all that, could he have rolled back the stone door from the inside of the tomb seeing that "it was exceeding great" (Mark 16:4)? Finally, in such an emaciated condition, what stretch of the imagination could envision that Jesus would have been able, if only a mere man, to have presented himself to the disciples on that very day as the picture of perfect health and divine power sufficient to inspire in them a confidence that he had triumphed over the power of death?

The problems created by substituting the speculations of prejudice for the facts of history are more difficult to believe than the resurrection.

The Significance of the Third Day

On the third day after the crucifixion—the first day of the week—Jesus' tomb was found empty (Matthew 28:1-7; Mark 16:1-7; Luke 24:1-7; John 20:1-7). This singular, historic fact offers at least five points of evidence for the resurrection.

Jesus Prophesied He Would Rise on the Third Day After Crucifixion

Christ specified that his would be a death by crucifixion (Matthew 20:19; John 3:14; 8:28; 12:32-33). The absence of his body from the tomb on the third day following that event becomes extremely significant for this reason: while Jesus stedfastly maintained that he would die by crucifixion, the Jews failed in repeated attempts to kill him by some other means. (See Luke 4:28-30; John 5:18; 7:1, 25; 8:59; 10:31; 11:8.) Thus, the fact of the empty tomb on the third day lends a great deal of credibility to the resurrection since both the kind of death and the very day of the resurrection were foretold throughout his entire ministry and since both events were fulfilled in spite of the Jews employing physical opposition to prevent their fulfillment. The question is, how could Jesus bring it off unless he was something more than a man?

The Prophecy Was Foretold Early in His Ministry

The idea that Jesus predicted his crucifixion only after he began to detect the direction that the stream of events were carrying him is contradicted in that he foretold it from the outset of his ministry. After the first temple cleansing, Jesus pointed to his resurrection (John 2:13-22). When challenged by the Pharisees to show them a sign of his deity, he appealed to Jonah's experience in the fish for three days and three nights as a sign prophetic of his own experience to be accomplished in his death, burial, and resurrection (Matthew 12:38-40). Here is a prophecy characteristic of the biblical kind, the fulfillment of which was so far removed from the time of the prophecy that it was humanly impossible to foretell.

The Prophecy Became Common Knowledge

The prophecy of death by crucifixion and of a resurrection on the third day spread beyond the circle of Jesus' disciples. The Jewish rulers knew of it and considered that the knowledge of the prophecy was so widespread among the common people as a sign of his messiahship that they took official steps to prevent his body from being taken from the tomb before the third day (Matthew 27:62-66).

It is rather clear that the Jews did not expect a resurrection to take place and their intentions were to present the lifeless body of Jesus on the third day as an absolute refutation of his messianic claims. Yet the body was not there on the third day!

An Empty Tomb on the Third Day

The tomb was both open and empty on the third day. Jesus' body was nowhere to be found. Had either the Roman or Jewish rulers removed the body at any time prior to the third day, it would have been no problem for either of them to have presented the corpse and to have stopped the new movement cold. Why didn't they do it? Simply because they had no knowledge of where the body was. All they knew for sure was that they had failed to keep the crucified Jesus in the tomb.

Christianity and the First Day of the Week

From the day of Pentecost following the crucifixion, the first day of the week has been special to Christians. The transfer of emphasis from the Sabbath day to the first day of the week is a very impressive testimony to the significance of this particular day, and more especially when we remember that devout Sabbath-keeping Jews who became Christians never questioned the correctness of this emphasis.

Nowhere in Scripture is it called a special day or even a holy day. But that it contained for the church a special significance is made clear in the Scriptures. On the first day of the week, the church was established (Acts 2:1-47). Paul shows us that the first day of the week had already become special to the church by the time he directed the Corinthians to begin regular collections on the first day of the week (1 Corinthians 16:1-2). And also, the church observed the Lord's supper on that day (Acts 20:7).

The question here is: What significant event happened to produce such an emphasis if not the resurrection of Jesus Christ?

Conclusion

If Jesus was raised from the dead, his claims are true and he is the Lord. If not, the historical Jesus who claimed to be God with the gift of eternal life was in reality a liar, a cheat, and a blasphemer.

But how can we know? We can know by the evidence. The facts are that there was a historical Jesus who was crucified on a Roman cross, who was buried, and whose tomb was found empty on the third day, even as he had foretold. If Jesus were not raised by the power of God, then what possible alternative can be suggested in answer to the facts as we have them? What reasonable alternative is there to the resurrection?

You do not have to throw away your mind to believe in Christ Jesus as Lord. It is a reasonable matter based on the evidence from historical documents. The function of reason is to sit in judgment on the evidence and to draw a conclusion which correctly answers to it. Reason demands an answer to the historical fact of Christ's empty tomb. What does the evidence say?

6

The Pentecost Phenomenon
The Resurrection of Jesus Christ (2)

I have yet many things to say unto you, but ye cannot bear them now. Howbeit when he, the Spirit of truth is come, he shall guide you into all the truth.

—Jesus to the Apostles

On the day of Pentecost following the crucifixion, a change of extreme proportions occurred within the apostles, permanently transforming them into utterly new men. From the third hour of the day—about 9 o'clock in the morning—their authoritative proclamation, their unity of knowledge and boldness of spirit stood in distinct contrast to their former lives before that day. Before Pentecost, they were fearful of the Jews, confused about the kingdom of God, uncertain of their purpose as apostles, and, on occasion, at odds with each other. But on

Pentecost, they were unified into a bold band of authoritative and knowledgeable preachers. They became fearless in spirit and dedicated in their purpose to preach the gospel to the whole creation. In only hours, they would assume the dynamic leadership of a new religion which would quickly cover the earth and persist through their teachings until the present time. In addition, they were empowered to speak the languages of all races. This can no more be denied than can the amazement of the Jews who stood in awesome wonder of it.

The throngs of Jews who had gathered in Jerusalem from various parts of the empire were stricken with the phenomenon and asked for an explanation (Acts 2:12). These events called for an explanation, because this renewal and empowerment of the apostles was immediate, not gradual. The answer they gave was that this phenomenon was due to the intervention of the Holy Spirit as Jesus had earlier promised.

Coming of the Spirit Is Proof of the Resurrection

Jesus had promised the apostles that after he ascended to heaven, he would send them the Holy Spirit. Then, within hours he was slain. If the promise was to be kept, Jesus would have to rise from the dead in order to go back to heaven and to send the Holy Spirit.

Due to the nature of the case, if it can be established that the change in the apostles was the result of the coming of the Holy Spirit, then the resurrection of Jesus, which was essential to his return to heaven, can be logically and historically sustained.

The Facts in the Case

Nothing is to be assumed regarding the resurrection evidence. Facts are essential in the development of the proposition. Therefore, ever keep in mind that the factual evidence coming to us from the New Testament is as historically reliable as that from any other ancient source considered to be reliable. There are five important facts from which the argument emerges.

Fact Number One: The Promised Mission of the Holy Spirit

Before his crucifixion, Jesus promised to his apostles that the Holy Spirit would come to them and endow them with a full knowledge of the gospel. He promised that the Holy Spirit would give them a perfect recollection of all that he had said to them during his personal ministry and that the Spirit would teach them all things which were inherent in that gospel ministry (John 14:26). He promised that the Holy Spirit would guide them into a total knowledge of all gospel truth, which at the particular time of the promise they could not have known: “I have yet many things to say unto you, but ye cannot bear them now. Howbeit when he, the Spirit of truth, is come, he shall guide you into all the truth” (John 16:12-13). The language unmistakably reveals that the promise was to be fulfilled by a supernatural intervention by the Holy Spirit, who would superimpose his own knowledge upon the apostles’ minds. The knowledge of the meaning of Christ’s life and death was to be an immediate gift, not a gradual process of learning.

Fact Number Two: The Coming of the Holy Spirit Was Conditional

Jesus imposed upon himself the condition of returning to the Father in heaven as a prerequisite to sending the Holy Spirit to the apostles: “Nevertheless I tell you the truth: It is expedient for you that I go away; for if I go not away, the Comforter will not come unto you; but if I go, I will send him unto you. And he, when he is come, will convict the world in respect of sin, and of righteousness, and of judgment: of sin, because they believe not on me; of righteousness, because I go to the Father” (John 16:7-10). His statement makes it clear that the Holy Spirit would not be able to come to the apostles until after he had returned to the Father.

Fact Number Three: Jesus Died On the Cross

Eyewitness testimony that Jesus died on the cross has been carefully documented by Matthew

(27:50) and John (19:30). Mark testified that the centurion in charge of the execution was convinced that Jesus died and so satisfied Pilate to grant the corpse to Joseph of Arimathaea for burial (Mark 15:39-45). John gave his eyewitness account that one of the soldiers of the execution squad pierced Jesus' side with a sword to the extent that both blood and water flowed out freely from the gaping wound (John 19:34-35). His preparation for burial and his entombment are thoroughly attested to by all of the gospel writers (Matthew 27:57-61; Mark 15:42-47; Luke 23:50-55; John 19:38-42).

Any suggestion that Jesus survived the ordeal of the cross and the spear to live out the rest of his life in some other area of the world, as claimed by some Hindus and Moslems, is without any historical basis and disregards four reliable testimonies to the fact of his death and burial.

The Force of the Argument

The facts thus far have brought Jesus to his death. Keep carefully in mind that Jesus promised to return to the Father in heaven before he could send the Holy Spirit to the apostles, but that he died before returning (John 20:17). Therefore, to ascend to the Father and dispatch the Holy Spirit, he would have to be raised from the dead. It is essential, therefore, to prove that the Holy Spirit came to the apostles and performed his work as promised in order to prove the resurrection of

Jesus. Our task in this instance is to show that the Holy Spirit accomplished his work upon the apostles and by this means established the resurrection claim to be true. The evidence that the Holy Spirit came on Pentecost and fulfilled his mission as Jesus had promised will be developed from the following facts.

Fact Number Four: The State of the Apostles Prior to Pentecost

During the ministry of Christ, the state of the apostles theologically, intellectually, positionally, emotionally, and educationally spans in extreme contrast to the superior level of excellence which they attained in each of these areas on Pentecost morning. When this phenomenon is coupled with the fact that it occurred within each of the apostles in no more time than it takes for a gust of wind to pass by, the claim of supernatural intervention cannot be easily discounted. Consider the pre-Pentecost state of the apostles.

1. *Theologically*

In a word, it was nationalistic. The Jewish concept of the prophecies of the kingdom was of a literal sort that viewed their nation to be bathed once again in Solomonic splendor, their Messiah-King to be enthroned in ultimate regal glory, and the power and influence of their Israelite dominion to be extended to the ends of the earth.

Their nationalistic view of the kingdom was demonstrated in their response to Christ's feeding the five thousand with but two fish from a lad's lunch sack and five loaves of barley bread. They interpreted the act as an ability to supply Jewish armies with food and weapons to throw off the Roman yoke and made an attempt to take him by force to make him their king (John 6:14-15). Christ's rejection of this overture highlights the distance between their theological expectations of Old Testament messianic prophecies and Christ's own messianic intent and purpose. This nationalistic view led the apostles to miss the redemptive purpose of Christ and to misunderstand his theology of the kingdom of God.

We recall the incident when Jesus asked his disciples saying, "Who say ye that I am?" and Peter responded that he was "the Christ (Messiah) the son of the living God" (Matthew 16:15-16). Then Jesus charged his disciples "that they should tell no man that he was the Christ" (v.20). It seems natural to ask why Jesus charged them to silence about his identity after eliciting this confession from them. But Jesus did not equate their confidence in him with an understanding of the true spiritual nature of his messiahship and so charged them to keep silent about it until they were better informed. That information would come at Pentecost.

Immediately following this discussion, Jesus began to explain that he was to go to Jerusalem and suffer death at the hands of the Jewish hierarchy. Once again, Peter responded that as long as he was anywhere near his Lord, he would do what he could to prevent anything like that from happening: "Be it far from thee, Lord: this shall never be unto thee." Christ's answer must have stabbed Peter to the heart; "Get thee behind me, Satan: thou art a stumbling block unto me: for thou mindest not the things of God, but the things of men" (Matthew 16:21-23). Human nature being what it is, Peter may well have wondered why Jesus asked them to confess him only to charge them to say nothing about it, and then why Jesus rebuked Peter, calling him Satan when he volunteered to lay down his life for his Lord! But while the words of Jesus were hard at the time, they exposed the nationalistic concept which Peter and the apostles had of Christ and of his kingdom. Therefore, Peter was minding the things of men and not the things of God.

On another occasion, two more of his apostles, spurred on by their mother's ambition for them, requested of Jesus seats of authority at Christ's right hand and left hand in the kingdom of God (Matthew 20:20-22; Mark 10:35-39). But Jesus countered: "Ye know not what ye ask," and so contrasted his own view of the kingdom with theirs.

This contrast of conceptions of the Messiah and his kingdom explains the amazement expressed by the disciples when Jesus proclaimed that it was easier for a camel to pass through the eye of a needle than for a rich man to enter into the kingdom of God (Matthew 19:24). Their own pre-Pentecost conception of the kingdom could not conceive of rich men not gaining access through their riches to the kingdom. *The spiritual nature of the kingdom was in Jesus' mind alone.* They simply were not able, at that time, to grapple with such statements as, "The kingdom of God cometh not with observation: neither shall they say, Lo, here! or, There! for lo, the kingdom of God is within you" (Luke 17:20-21).

An impressive incident following the crucifixion serves to illustrate the Jewish view of the messianic kingdom which they interpreted strictly in terms of partisan Israelite nationalism. Two of Jesus' disciples were despairing that their messianic hopes had been blasted by the crucifixion of Jesus and so they gave as the reason for their sadness that they had "hoped that it was he who should redeem Israel" (Luke 24:13-21). Their conception of the redemption of Israel did not come close to the spiritual idea of a kingdom composed of regenerated men saved by the blood of a crucified king. At that moment, the idea of a kingdom brought into existence by the death of their king was incomprehensible. Redemption from sin would soon replace their present idea; but for the moment, their desire was for the redemption of their nation from its low position under Roman domination to the national glory which they believed would be the fulfillment of their messianic prophecies.

Pentecost was only a few days away; until then their nationalistic concept of the kingdom of God would persist. Even though they had their Scriptures interpreted to them as being fulfilled in a redemptive context (Luke 24:25-27, 44-47), they did not take hold of the spiritual meaning. Even after the resurrection, Jesus clearly stated that what he had told them throughout his ministry was exactly what he would tell them now: that the Scriptures were fulfilled in his death, burial, and resurrection and that, as a result, repentance and remission of sins would be preached in his name to all the nations (Luke 24:44-47). Yet they did not fully understand and wouldn't until Pentecost. Even at the empty tomb, they did not know of the Scriptures which foretold the resurrection (John 20:9).

This explains Jesus' words in John 16:12-13, "I have yet many things to say unto you, but ye cannot bear them now. Howbeit when he, the Spirit of truth, is come, he shall guide you into all the truth." The apostles had been blocked from a spiritual view of the kingdom of God by their nationalistic theology. On the day of Pentecost, their view was drastically changed.

2. *Intellectually*

The apostles were rather dull of perception prior to Pentecost regarding a number of Christ's statements concerning the kingdom and his messianic intent and purpose. After two occasions of feeding multitudes with loaves and fishes, hardly adequate for one person (Matt. 14:15-21; 15:32-38), he told his disciples, "take heed and beware the leaven of the Pharisees and Sadducees" (Matt. 16:6). Immediately, the disciples began to talk about their failure to bring bread to eat. Jesus then asked why they didn't perceive that he wasn't talking about bread. He could have produced more bread as easily as he did when he fed the multitudes. Then, after another explanation about their lack of perception about the leaven of the Pharisees and Sadducees, they understood that he warned them against their particular doctrine. On another occasion (Luke 18:31-34) Jesus plainly told them that he would fulfill the Scripture in his death, burial, and resurrection at Jerusalem and would rise again on the third day. But "they perceived not the things that were said." They just did not grasp his meaning.

3. *Positionally*

The apostles were ambitious for seats of power in the coming kingdom (Matt. 20:20-28). As they jockeyed for position, they divided their ranks with jealous indignation. On the very eve of the crucifixion, they contended with each other as to who was greatest (Luke 22:24-30). They were not united in relation to each other.

4. *Emotionally*

Jesus told his disciples that at his crucifixion, they would be scattered abroad like sheep and that Peter would deny him three times before the cock finished crowing (Matt. 26:31-34). All the disciples were adamant that they would not deny their Lord; and at the time Jesus was arrested, it seems they tried to make good their boast. But their bravery turned to fear as they beheld the overwhelming flow of circumstances against them, and they fled (Matt. 26:35-56). Peter's fear led him to deny Christ, just as Jesus had predicted (Mark 14:66-72). On the third day after the crucifixion, all except Thomas quietly secured themselves behind closed doors "for fear of the Jews" (John 20:19). These men were not cowards, but the natural emotion of fear gripped them at the crucifixion events.

5. *Educationally*

The apostles were not educated in rabbinical training, which is reminiscent of the statements made by the Jewish leaders about Jesus in John 7:14-15. Therefore, they could not know the minutiae of oral law or be expected to engage in Scripture argumentation as of the Law. Luke is clear on this point (Acts 4:13).

Taken as a whole, the state of the apostles prior to Pentecost would not produce any expectation that this disorganized band of inept men could assume the dynamic leadership of a new movement that was soon to catch the attention of the entire Roman Empire and persist with millions of adherents for the next two thousand years.

Fact Number Five: The Change at Pentecost

Luke records the drastic change which took place within the apostles on Pentecost morning and claims that it was due to the coming of the Holy Spirit (Acts 2:1-4). Barely fifty days had passed from the event at Calvary to Pentecost. Suddenly, on that day, they were transformed.

Their theology was now redemptive rather than nationalistic. They no longer cringed at the thought of Christ's death on the cross. They preached the necessity of their messiah's death for Israel's redemption, which now they knew was in the forgiveness of their sins. They no longer anticipated national prosperity and worldwide glory. They no longer interpreted messianic prophecy in terms of the redemption of the Jewish nation from their inglorious position of being just one more nation under the sway of Rome. They preached that prophecy was fulfilled in the death, burial, and resurrection of Jesus and in the resulting salvation from sin, death and hell and in the establishment of the Kingdom of God. Intellectually, they were sharp, speaking confidently of the resurrection and lordship of Jesus with the authority that comes from knowledge and conviction. They spoke fluently in the multitude of dialects and languages that represented the different nationalities that had converged upon Jerusalem for the feast of Pentecost. No longer were they at odds with each other, but were united upon a common faith with a single redemptive purpose. They were emboldened to the amazement of the multitudes, fearlessly proclaiming their message as the fulfillment of Old Testament prophecy. And without exception, they maintained their doctirnal position and newly acquired capabilities through ensuing persecution. Here was a change of such proportions that the mind is boggled to think of it happening so quickly. Yet, it is one of the facts of history.

Was the Change Natural or Supernatural?

This fact of history must be explained. The question to be answered is: What processes combined to produce this phenomenon, this change in these Galileans in such a brief moment of time? Luke claimed it was the coming of the Holy Spirit (Acts 2:1-4). So did the apostles (1 Corinthians 2:6-10; Ephesians 3:3-5; 1 Peter 1:12). But inasmuch as the Holy Spirit could not have come to the apostles until after Jesus had ascended back to the Father, and since Jesus had been crucified, it follows that for the Spirit to have come on Pentecost, Jesus had to have been raised from the dead.

Can the Pentecost Phenomenon Be Explained by Natural Causes?

The only alternative explanation to the one offered in the New Testament is that the change in the apostles was caused by natural processes. But, what natural processes could have possibly combined to produce such a radical change in so short a period of time? The two essential ingredients required to produce such a thorough-going change in religious concept and thought patterns and linguistic ability are time and education. But the fact is that the time essentially required for an educational process to produce such an effect as this one was absolutely not available. A mere ten days had lapsed since they manifested their utter confusion about Christ's purpose and their future (Acts 1:6).

If the time normally required was not available, how, then, was the change produced? At the same time, we must ask who their teacher would have been? Who was able to unify them in both concept and spirit in that scant moment of time before Pentecost? How can we explain the exegesis, the arrangement, and adoption of the great mass of apostolic doctrine which interpreted Old Testament prophecy as fulfilled in Christianity? The concept which the apostles preached from Pentecost was not theirs ten days earlier. Is it reasonable to believe that in ten days the apostles could have assimilated and categorized that great volume of doctrine for the church to continue in (Acts 2:42), to successfully relate it to the Scriptures of the Old Testament, all in perfect accord with one another and without a dissenting voice among them, and to have done it all by mere human effort?

Natural processes certainly do not appear adequate to satisfy the question before us as to the cause for that change at Pentecost. Since neither the time nor the teacher can be found to satisfy the natural processes required for that change, then, what is unintelligent in the belief that the cause was supernatural?

Only a Supernatural Answer Is Consistent With the Facts

The explanation that the Holy Spirit came and superimposed himself with his knowledge and power upon the apostles perfectly corresponds with the facts in this unique situation. This is the only explanation that harmonizes with the fact that Jesus promised the Spirit's coming, that harmonizes with the fact of the apostles' radical change, and with the fact that the apostles and Luke claimed that the change was due to the Spirit's coming and supernatural guidance.

Conclusion

We are left with a fact and a question. The fact is: The apostles changed drastically on the day of Pentecost, and natural processes cannot explain that change. The question is: Was it a natural or a supernatural change? The only reasonable answer in keeping with the facts lies in the resurrection of Jesus Christ. It is reasonable to believe that the Holy Spirit came from God and endowed the apostles, for their change came in a moment of time, entirely too fast for the natural course of things to produce it. And inasmuch as the crucified Jesus was not to send the Holy Spirit to accomplish this change until he had returned to the Father, it is also reasonable to believe that Jesus Christ was therefore raised from the dead, that he ascended to heaven, and that he sent the Holy Spirit who produced this great phenomenon at Pentecost. Based on the facts as we have them, this is a very reasonable conclusion.

7

The Testimony of the Twelve
The Resurrection of Jesus Christ (3)

This Jesus did God raise up, whereof we are all witnesses.

—Peter for the apostles

Believing Without Seeing Is Not Blind Faith

We see Christ through the mind's eye. What we see is his life and death and resurrection. The way we see is through the wonderful medium of historical testimony. For an illustration, the apostle Thomas became so extremely pessimistic about Christ that even after the other apostles had testified to him that they had seen Jesus alive, he set his own conditions for believing. He said, "Except I shall see in his hands the print of the nails, and put my finger into the print of the nails, and put my hand into his side, I will not believe" (John 20:25). Then John tells us his eyewitness account of how eight days later Jesus met with Thomas and gave him the opportunity to test the resurrection evidence for himself. He wrote that after Thomas had seen the evidence and had been invited to test its genuineness for himself by putting his finger into the nail prints of the cross and his hand into the gaping wound in his side, he humbly confessed that Jesus was both his Lord and his God.

That was the most blasphemous thing a Jew could say to another man, unless what he said was true. It's pretty clear that Thomas was convinced that Jesus was the son of God. Then, at that moment, Jesus answered Thomas in words which stretch right up to us today: "Because thou hast seen me thou hast believed: blessed are they that have not seen, and yet have believed" (John 20:26-29). Right there Jesus spoke about believing without seeing.

Now the question is asked today: Why should we believe in Jesus when we have not seen anything? How can we know for sure that Jesus even lived, much less was raised from the dead, when we are separated from those events by nearly twenty centuries? The answer to that is testimony.

Belief in Christ Is Based on the Apostles' Testimony

It is a mistake to think that the historic faith of the Christian religion was begun or maintained by emotional subjectivism, that is, by following after one's inner feelings as an evidence that God has spoken to us or that Christ was raised from the dead. Jesus made it clear that the basis for believing in him rested solidly on the apostles' word (John 17:20). That is because their word was a testimony to what they themselves had seen and heard and experienced with Christ for the three and a half years they were with him. Their word was the testimony of eyewitnesses. That is how we know about the incident between Jesus and Thomas; John was there and witnessed it and told us about it in his written testimony.

The Christian faith (the objective religious system), like the Christian's personal faith, is based squarely on those objective, historical events to which those eyewitnesses like Thomas, a few days later at Pentecost, directed men's attention. It was this basis on which Peter encouraged persecuted Christians in the first century to endure the fiery test of their faith in Christ, of whom he said "not having seen ye love; on whom, though now ye see him not, yet believing, ye rejoice greatly with joy unspeakable" (1 Peter 1:6-8). Theirs was not a blind faith. It rested on the testimony of eyewitnesses like Thomas and Peter, whose reliability, as far as they were concerned, was unimpeachable (2 Peter 1:16). So great was the power of their apostolic testimony for the resurrection of Christ that those early Christians loved him even though they had never seen him.

Our Identity With First Century Men

Today's man stands right where most first century men stood—totally without sight and sound of Jesus Christ. This is where modern men, though removed from Jesus of Nazareth by nearly two thousand years, can find the point of contact with nearly all of those first century Christians and their indomitable faith. We have not seen Jesus in the flesh, much less have we had opportunity to examine the resurrection evidences in his hands and side to see for ourselves whether the prints of the cross were fact or faked. But, then, neither had those persecuted believers to whom Peter sent his epistle of encouragement (1 Peter 1:8). But they believed because of the apostles' eyewitness testimony to the historical facts of his death and resurrection.

Look at Theophilus. He was the Roman official to whom Luke wrote both his gospel account and the book of Acts. Theophilus stood in the same place where we stand right now, he had not seen Jesus in the flesh, nor had any apostle come to him with a confirmation of the gospel by miracles. Like any number of modern men, he had learned somewhat of Jesus, but needed confirmation in order to believe it. Luke arranged the apostles' testimony in written form, in true historiographical style, so that Theophilus could have a confirmation of the gospel he needed, as Luke stated it, "that thou mightest know the certainty concerning the things wherein thou wast instructed" (Luke 1:4). What we have today is what Theophilus had then. He had a witness to Jesus in written form, and we have that same witness, the historically verified and totally reliable books of Luke and Acts. So we stand where Theophilus stood in relation to the historical truth of Christ; and with those written witnesses, we can be as certain of the gospel as he could.

The New Testament Idea of Witnessing

Luke wrote that "with great power gave the apostles their witness of the resurrection of the Lord Jesus: and great grace was upon them all" (Acts 4:33). The convincing power of that apostolic witness was so great that it resulted in the production of great faith among all those that heard. Something stirring and convincing was present in that first century testimony by the apostles which brought multitudes to belief in Christ in all parts of the world.

Modern "Witnessing"

No one today has the power to witness for Christ inasmuch as none of us has seen anything of him to which we can bear objective testimony. Today's references to bearing witness for Christ are usually misnomers. Generally, that means that someone's own personal experience is supposed to have become a bonafide testimony to the present power of Christ in their lives. But such "witnessing" is a totally subjective approach and has no better proof than some believer's statement that Jesus or the Holy Spirit is the power behind some experience. It cannot be proven to be more than human impulses subjectively interpreted as the leading of the Holy Spirit. We would not deny that experiences are happening to people which have a special meaning to them, even ecstatic speaking. However, Hindus, who do not believe in Jesus as Saviour, also speak ecstatically and hold out their "experience" as a witness to the empowering help offered by Krishna. Are we therefore to believe that this is bonafide testimony that Krishna is a living god? Such testimony proves nothing. Today's "testimonies" of personal experiences with Christ appear to be the subjective interpretations which each person places on a happening or feeling he had. What this kind of witness amounts to is no more than what some individual thinks has happened to him. This is not the New Testament idea of witnessing.

The Purpose of the Apostles' Testimony

Jesus said that the apostles would bear witness of him (John 15:27). To bear witness means to give testimony in behalf of something with a view toward the confirmation of its truthfulness, its reality. The grand truth to which the apostles would bear witness for Christ was to his resurrection. They did this by stating that they themselves saw Jesus alive after the crucifixion; that for forty days after his resurrection, they had a daily opportunity to examine him closely, to handle his flesh and to examine the scars of the cross and so to satisfy themselves that this was the same person with whom they had walked for over three years prior to his death at Calvary. This testimony was to their own objective experiences with the risen Christ.

The apostles' sermons in the book of Acts reveal the characteristic line of their apologetic thrust. On Pentecost they stood up to give their testimony to the fact that Jesus of Nazareth was the resurrected and living Christ. Their proposition was that Jesus, whom the Jews had slain, had been raised from the dead (Acts 2:22-24). Peter affirmed that "this Jesus did God raise up, whereof we are all witnesses" (v. 32). Their claim to be witnesses of Jesus after the resurrection was offered as a proof to those who had not seen him alive. Later, Peter and John preached to another large crowd of Jews who had consented to the death of Jesus. The apostles testified that they had "killed the Prince of life; whom God raised from the dead; whereof we are witnesses" (Acts 3:15). They were arrested by the ruling Jews for this testimony and were brought before the council who commanded them not to speak in the name of Christ again. But they responded that they could not but speak the things which they had seen and heard! (Acts 4:19-20). They insisted that they had actually seen and heard Jesus Christ after the resurrection. After a warning from the Sanhedrin not to preach in Jesus' name again, they were released. But true to their commission, they returned to their work of preaching and testifying that Jesus was raised. Consequently, they were arrested again. Brought back to the Jewish council, the high priest sternly reminded them:

> *We strictly charged you not to teach in this name: and behold you have filled Jerusalem with your teaching, and intend to bring this man's blood upon us. But Peter and the apostles answered and said, We must obey God rather than men. The God of our fathers raised up Jesus, whom ye slew, hanging him on a tree. . . . And we are witnesses of these things.* (Acts 5:28-32)

One convincing evidence that Jesus had indeed been raised was that all twelve of the apostles, even though under threats from the hierarchy—who very well held the power to pass the death sentence—nevertheless persisted in their preaching that the resurrection was a fact and that they were eyewitnesses of the risen Christ. To them, the implications of that event were such that they could not stop preaching it though it would cost them their lives.

The same methodology was used when preaching to Gentiles. To the centurion, Cornelius, Peter preached as always that the apostles were "witnesses of all things which he [Jesus] did in the country of the Jews, and in Jerusalem; whom also they slew, hanging him on a tree. Him God raised up the third day, and gave him to be made manifest, not to all the people, but unto witnesses that were chosen before of God, even to us, who ate and drank with him after he rose from the dead" (Acts 10:39-41). In one of his sermons, Paul pointed out that the original apostles carried in their testimony the proof of the resurrection. He reported that "God raised him from the dead: and he was seen for many days of them that came up with him from Galilee to Jerusalem, who are now his witnesses unto the people" (Acts 13:30-31). Paul's own testimony in Athens was that God would bring them all into judgment and that he had given assurance of this to all men "in that he hath raised him from the dead" (Acts 17:31).

Luke's account of the apostles' presentation of the resurrection is presented with such startling objectivity that we are impressed with the fact that they actually expected their listeners to believe them. In each recorded case of preaching Christ, the apostles presented the death, burial, and resurrection as historical truth and then offered their own eyewitness testimony as proof of their claim.

John's Claim for the Apostles

This same idea is presented in 1 John 1:1-4, though perhaps at first the fact that the resurrection is implied does not appear.

> *That which was from the beginning, that which we have heard, that which we have seen with our eyes, that which we beheld, and our hands handled, concerning the Word of life (and the life was manifested, and we have seen, and bear witness, and declare unto you the life, the eternal life, which was with the Father, and was manifested unto us); that which we have seen and heard declare we unto you also, that ye also may have fellowship with us.*

John represents the entire body of the apostles by using the plural pronouns *we* and *our*. When he spoke of "that which we have heard . . . which we have seen with our eyes . . . which we beheld . . . our hands handled," he was speaking of the resurrected Lord whom the apostles had seen and heard. Then he explained that in this way, the eternal life was made known to them. How else can eternal life be made known to mortal man? He is born to live but a few years, then dies. Only a resurrection can prove to dying mankind that there is an eternal life. The apostle John stated that all the apostles bore witness to Christ's historical, bodily resurrection and its confirmation of eternal life. This was their constant and never-ending claim from Pentecost.

The Power of the Apostles' Testimony

Those ingredients which combined to give credibility to the apostles' claim for the resurrection were the number of the eyewitnesses to the fact, their unity of doctrine, and their faithful lives in persecution.

Their Number

Paul's testimony was unique to that of the original apostles. His personal encounter with Christ was not like theirs, and, therefore, his account would be different from theirs. (His testimony will be considered in chapter eight.) At this point, we want to consider the power which the twelve exercised. Usually, one person of reliable character is sufficient to confirm the claim or the character of another. In the case for the resurrection of Jesus, there were twelve witnesses whose reliability is confirmed by their lives in hardship and persecution, which was due to their resurrection claim, and whose lives, which were consistent with their gospel, exonerated them from any indictment that their testimony was due to some ulterior motive. Twelve such witnesses would be considered more than adequate in any court. If twelve would not be received as confirmation of the resurrection, neither would the testimony of twelve hundred. The unvarying testimony of twelve is a reasonable number.

Their Unity

Unity of agreement among the total number of witnesses lends the greatest credibility to a claim, regardless of the extremities to which the claim may reach. In the apostles' case, their eyewitness observations were extended over a pre-crucifixion period of some three and a half years and a post-crucifixion period of another forty days to determine that this was the same Jesus in both ministries. Inasmuch as their testimony to the life of Christ, his death, his resurrection, and his post-resurrection appearances are in agreement, and since their doctrine in every phase of the Christian faith agrees, and since all the apostles were willing to suffer the most miserable of persecutions for what they claimed they had seen and heard, we can be assured of having the best possible evidence.

Their Lives

Doubtless, the faithfulness of the apostles was the crucible of the Christian religion. From the beginning, the grand evidence for the resurrection was the unswerving testimony of a unified band of fearless men. Even though these men were imprisoned (Acts 4:1-3; 5:18, 25) and threatened with their lives (Acts 4:17, 21; 5:17-33), and in spite of the early martyrdom of the apostle James (Acts 12:1-3), they maintained that they had seen Jesus alive after the crucifixion and that they had walked with him for another forty days. They persisted, without variation from their course both doctrinally and morally, in the face of severe hardship, even to the death. It goes without saying that it is against human nature for such lives as those apostles lived to be based upon a lie. You cannot expect that of human nature.

Today we have no testimony of our own experience that can be legitimately offered as proof of Christ's resurrection. Our testimony must be that of the apostles. The apostolic testimony, as recorded in the New Testament, is the intended ground of belief for all time to come (Luke 24:44-48; John 17:20). This apostolic testimony was the testimony of those early Christians who had not seen the Lord (Revelation 12:11). It is not ours to offer any "experiences" of our own as proof of Christianity's reliability. Ours today is to preach the word of qualified witnesses (2 Timothy 4:1-2).

Conclusion

A very reasonable conclusion in view of the evidence as it comes to us in the historical documents of the New Testament is that what the apostles testified to actually happened: Jesus was raised, and they saw him even as they claimed. Their motives were not challenged. Their lives were consistent with their doctrine. What other answer can be offered for the lives and teaching of the twelve apostles, without contradicting the facts? Here, in the number of the witnesses, their unity, and their lives, lies the real force of Luke's words that "with great power gave the apostles their witness of the resurrection of the Lord Jesus." The eyewitness testimony of the apostles was the power that brought great grace upon them all.

8

From Fanaticism to Faith
The Resurrection of Jesus Christ (4)

For the king knoweth of these things . . . for this hath not been done in a corner.
—Paul to Agrippa

Paul States His Case

Luke tells us that after two full years in jail at Caesarea, Paul, the prisoner, was at last given an opportunity to defend himself before king Agrippa against the slanderous charges of the Jews that he was seditious (Acts 26:1-7). He stood in chains before an impressive assembly of military officers and Roman nobility which had been arranged by the regional governor, Festus, at the arrival of king Agrippa. To these, the apostle related the evidence for the resurrection of Jesus Christ and informed them that his preaching of this gospel, which he claimed was the fulfillment of the Jewish messianic hope, was the real reason for the Jew's opposition to him. The conflict which existed between their theology and his, Paul said, was the real reason back of their attempts to make it appear as if he were a political dissident.

Paul began his apologetic by recounting the fact that from his youth to his conversion he lived the strict life of a Pharisee. He then challenged Agrippa to admit that it is not incredible for God to raise the dead (v. 8). He proceeded to paint a picture of his anti-Christian manner of life before his conversion and the severity to which his opposition extended against the church. The force of his argument for the resurrection was in that former manner of life, which was so furiously opposed to Christianity, and the fact of his unbelievable conversion. Paul's zeal against all Christians was of such a severe nature that any attempt by a Christian to convert him would have been suicidal. He was completely out of reach by any human effort to convert him to Christ. Yet, the fact is, he was converted.

A Great Contrast

The abruptness of the change from Paul's pre-Christian life as self-appointed exterminator of the Christian religion to zealous exponent of the gospel reveals a contrast of such proportions that natural causes are totally inadequate to explain them. His drastic change from persecutor of the church to preacher of Christ involved such extremes that his conversion could only have been produced by some force greater than any human could have exercised. It was Paul's claim that this phase of his life was reversed when Jesus appeared to him en route to Damascus and stopped him dead in his tracks. But since Jesus had been crucified prior to that incident, it was essential that he had to be raised from the dead in order to make that appearance.

PAUL'S THREE-PRONGED ARGUMENT

All of the facts are laid out in the New Testament in four separate accounts of Paul's conversion. The unique circumstances surrounding his manner of life in Judaism as a persecutor and the fact of his conversion to Christ set forth the structural material which forms a convincing apologetic for the resurrection. The material is arranged and presented three times in the book of Acts in chapters 9, 22, and 26. Paul himself arranges the same material in the Galatian letter to prove to the churches of Galatia that he had received his gospel directly from Jesus—not from man. Then he pointed to his former manner of life in the Jew's religion as a persecutor of the church to prove his claim. Inherent in the argument was the proof for the resurrection. It is this arrangement of the facts, which Paul related to the Galatians, that we will consider as evidence for the resurrection.

> *For I make known to you, brethren, as touching the gospel which was preached by me, that it is not after man. For neither did I receive it from man, nor was I taught it, but it came to me through revelation of Jesus Christ. For ye have heard of my manner of life in time past in the Jews' religion, how that beyond measure I persecuted the church of God, and made havoc of it: and I advanced in the Jews' religion beyond many of mine own age among my countrymen, being more exceedingly zealous for the traditions of my fathers.* (Galatians 1:11-14)

Notice carefully the inherent evidence for the resurrection. It is a matter of historical record that Jesus was crucified before Paul was converted. Jesus would therefore have to have been raised in order to appear to Paul personally and deliver the gospel to him. The evidence for this is laid out by Paul in a logical three-pronged argument from his former manner of life. This unique presentation is designed to impress upon us that his religious training from his youth, his education in the Scriptures as interpreted by his Pharisaical fathers, his success and prominence among those of his nation, and his zeal for what he was convinced was right had so thoroughly biased him against Christianity that his conversion to Christ would have been impossible to bring about by any *human* efforts. Only Christ himself could have approached this fiery persecutor to bring him to his knees and to His service.

1. His Fanatical Persecution

The evidence that Paul received the gospel from Jesus lies in the fierceness of his persecution. The phrase "beyond measure" stressed the severity of his persecution. This description of his former life was apparently well known to the Galatians. It seems he had only to mention that he had persecuted the church beyond measure for them to fully appreciate what he meant. Fortunately, Luke's history allows us to reconstruct a very clear picture of that persecution and of the character of the person behind it.

Luke introduces Saul of Tarsus as the instigator of Stephen's death and of an ensuing great persecution against the church (Acts 7:58-8:1). From that time, Saul laid waste the church, violently entering the homes of the disciples and dragging both men and women to confinement in prisons (Acts 8:3; 26:10). The fierce personal feelings he had against them is graphically described in the statement that "Saul, yet breathing threatening and slaughter against the disciples of the Lord, went unto the high priest, and asked of him letters to Damascus unto the synagogues, that if he found any that were of the Way, whether men or women, he might bring them bound to Jerusalem" (Acts 9:1-2). The persecution was so hot and Saul was so dedicated to it that some in Damascus who heard of his conversion expressed amazement that he could ever have been brought to Christ at all, especially since his intentions were to capture as many disciples as he could find and bring them bound to the chief priests at Jerusalem (Acts 9:20-21).

Years later in Jerusalem, in retelling his conversion, he revealed that his intentions were to deal the deathblow to Christianity (Acts 22:4), to make a scorched earth of the church of Christ. In his defense before Agrippa he recounted how, with complete consent of conscience, he shut up many of the saints in prisons, cast his vote for their death sentence, punished them even in their worship assemblies, and strained to make them blaspheme—as he judged it—by confessing their belief that Jesus is Lord (Acts 26:9-13). He capped his description of the extreme measure to which he carried his persecution by relating how he pressed on toward Damascus in the heat of the midday. While others rested during this time, he pushed his troops onward.

The Emerging Portrait of a Fanatic

From this historical account of Saul's persecution of the church emerges a picture of a persecutor so fierce, and at the same time spurred on by the religious conviction that what he was doing was right (Acts 26:9), that we are compelled to view him as fanatical in his opposition to Christianity.

He went beyond the measure of what we would normally expect from one who stood opposed to another's religion. It reached the measure of fanaticism. That is what Paul meant when he reminded the Galatians that he had persecuted the church beyond measure. And they fully understood it. Beyond measure! A fanatic!

The question at this point is: How do you deal with a fanatic? It's unlikely that a zealot would be won to the cause he opposes. This was Paul's point: No one could have won him to Christ, yet, he became a Christian. But, who converted him? Christians were unable to do so and Jews certainly would not have done it. Who, then, if not Christ? Paul confidently maintained that Christ Jesus appeared to him outside Damascus and directed him into the city to a residence where for three more days he taught the blinded persecutor and finally effected his conversion. But Christ was killed, crucified at Calvary. To make that appearance to Paul, he had to have been raised from the dead. What alternative answer is there which does not at some point contradict or disregard some of the facts in this case?

2. His Prominence Among the Jews

Paul said that he advanced in the Jews' religion beyond many of his own age. Several New Testament references reflect that advancement and give us information enabling us to determine the force of this second prong in his argument.

At least four areas of that advancement can be identified. First, he had advanced in *scholarship*, having had the famous Gamaliel for his teacher (Acts 22:3). His instructions as a Pharisee would distinguish him among his countrymen. Second, he advanced *financially* to some appreciable degree. It was necessary that he have some access to the funds of the temple treasury in order to carry out his police action, unless he was himself a man of some means. In either case, his exploits against the church required some sort of financial backing. Third, he advanced *socially*. His Roman citizenship, his birth and rearing in the house of a Pharisee, together with his education and zeal combined with other advantages to bring young Saul of Tarsus into contact with those officials in Judaism who were willing to grant him authority to carry on his campaign against Christians at Damascus. Fourth, he also advanced *to a position of power*. The authority and commission of the chief priests gave him power over the lives of the Christians whom he captured (Acts 26:12).

These four areas are sufficient to identify Paul's advancement to a place of *prominence* among the Jews. His reputation even preceeded him to Gentile officials a time or two (Acts 26:24). His prominence was outstanding among his nation. His point to the Galatians was that his prominence, coupled with his fanaticism, stood stubbornly in the way of any attempt to win him over to Christ.

So severe and powerful was he that fear struck the heart of Ananias, the disciple whom the Lord commissioned to baptize him (Acts 9:13-14). His prominent station, plus what he considered a divine sanction to eradicate Christianity (Acts 26:9), made conversion to Christ by any human being an utter impossibility.

What possible motive could brilliant young Saul of Tarsus have had for becoming a Christian if he had not actually seen Jesus as he said he did? What could Christians have possibly offered him as an incentive to make the change? To become a Christian for Saul of Tarsus meant a complete renunciation of all he counted to be meaningful and right from the days of his youth. Only an experience equal to an encounter with the resurrected Lord himself could have been adequate to do to him what in fact was done! But Jesus had been executed and buried in Jerusalem. How could he have won this outstanding Jew unless he had indeed been raised from the dead? Echo answers, how?

3. His Pharisaic Zeal and Prejudice

The final statement of evidence from Paul's former manner of life in Judaism was that he was "exceedingly zealous for the traditions of my fathers." The thing for which he was zealous is the key to this prong of his threefold argument. His fathers were the Pharisees whose traditions he was zealous to observe. He accepted their interpretations of the Law and the Prophets, which made it difficult to consider the Christian religion objectively. Though deeply sincere, Saul was tainted with the characteristic trait of the Pharisee—prejudice.

One can be honestly prejudiced, thinking in all sincerity that he possesses the truth. Saul was not mentally tormented as though he had second thoughts about his severe measures against Christians. His conscience was clear. He thought he was right. As he later reflected, "I verily thought with myself that I ought to do many things contrary to the name of Jesus of Nazareth" (Acts 26:9). His excess of zeal stemmed from his religious sincerity and dedication of purpose. Like cream coming to the top, we see in Saul of Tarsus the emergence of a certain religious *prejudice*.

The unreachable condition of this prominent fanatic would be greatly compounded by his peculiar religious prejudice. Only an event of extreme measure sufficient to match the extreme measures of Saul himself could have broken through that unique combination to win his mind and heart and life. But what forces can combine to convert a prejudiced, prominent fanatic? What processes can we conceive to have existed which could have so bent the mind and spirit of Saul, persuaded as he was that he was right? The challenge was compounded to the point of human inability to win this man to Christ. Yet he was won! Saul became a disciple of

Christ. The impossible happened. And it is a matter of historical fact, not fantasy, as fantastic as it may seem. But who did it? If it could not have been a man, then it could only have been the Lord. This is what Paul unstintingly claimed, until sometime in the year A.D. 68, Nero's executioner brought his earthly life to a close. If this were not the case, then what alternative in keeping with the facts can satisfy the historical fact of that radical reversal? Is it, after all, unintelligent in view of these historical facts to believe that Jesus was literally raised from the dead? Is it not as logical and reasonable a deduction as modern man can draw from a factual basis?

Alternatives to the Resurrection

It has been established that there was a real Saul of Tarsus whose life was as colorful and adventurous as the New Testament describes. The well-vindicated historian, Luke, wrote much in his book of Acts about Paul's life, often from the vantage point of an eyewitness since he had been the traveling companion of the great apostle on several journeys.[41] There are thirteen epistles which bear Paul's name. Even the most radical of liberal schools do not deny him the authorship of Romans,

41. In Acts there are several references to what are called the "we" passages where Luke includes himself in the company of the ones about whom he writes. Note the use of "we" and "us" in Acts 16:10-17; 20:5-15; 21:1-8; 27:1-28:16. See also Paul's reference to Luke's companionship in Colossians 4:14.

1 and 2 Corinthians, and Galatians. Historians have never doubted his historicity and his meetings with the other apostles. There is no doubt about it—Paul was as real a person of history, as testimony can verify.

Modernistic "Explanations" of Saul's Conversion

Modern man is gullible. He's not beyond worrying about modernistic suggestions that there may be alternative explanations for Saul's conversion other than the resurrection. Yet, invariably these "explanations" contradict known facts in the case. It has been suggested, for example, that Saul may have secretly harbored a deep sense of guilt for his terrible cruelties inflicted on Christians, that perhaps deep remorse had taken hold of him as he contemplated his purpose at Damascus, and that a possible stroke of heat lightning, coupled with the strength of the desert sun, acted by accumulation upon a possibly epileptic body and a tortured mind to bring to culmination the half-conscious process by which Saul thought he saw the resurrected Christ![42]

Examine the basis of this alternative explanation. It is sheer assumption without evidence and is prefaced by "maybe," "perhaps," "possibly." It completely disregards the fact that Paul's conscience was pronounced clear in his persecutions

42. Will Durant, *Caesar and Christ*, p. 581.

(Acts 23:1; 26:9). He affirmed that he had always lived before God with a clear conscience and that his opposition to Christianity was carried on in a manner that he thought before God was right and acceptable. He was certainly not plagued by a guilty conscience. He was doing, as he said, what he thought he ought to be doing (Acts 26:9).

A distinct characteristic of the unreasonable nature of liberalism is thus seen in its double-dealing with the Scriptures. First, the New Testament is considered by liberals to be sufficiently trustworthy to tell us of the historical reality of Saul and of his conversion, of the reality of his persecution, of his journey toward Damascus, and of the flash of light that left him blind.

But then his critics, without offering any historical evidence for their reasoning, discredit this same historical source of information right at the point where it relates the cause for that conversion—the appearance and further teaching by the risen Lord. From there, liberalism reconstructs another and totally different succession of events which are contrary to Luke's account and seeks to lead us to a conclusion entirely different from the one recorded by the historian. And what evidence is offered for the rejection of Luke's history at the point of Christ's appearance? Not a shred. What evidence is offered for the historical reliability of the alternate explanation? None. The consequent indictment is that Luke was an unreliable historian. With that kind of "alternative explanation" we could make out a case against Napoleon's defeat at Waterloo and suggest that "maybe," "perhaps," the real facts in the matter might "possibly" lead us to conclude that Bonaparte was shot at Bunker Hill!

How can this kind of biblical criticism lead a logical mind to a moment's doubt of the truthfulness of the biblical history? The modern man who thinks for himself will be driven to the conclusion that back of such criticism is a prejudice that Jesus could not have been raised from the dead, regardless of what the evidence from history may say.

Let us consider some more probable alternatives to the resurrection appearance to Saul and note the points of departure from the facts in each case.

Was Paul an Imposter?

If he perpetrated a hoax, what was the real reason for his drastic and life-long change from Judaism to Christianity? This leads logically to the motive for the change. If he invented the account, he would have to have had some reason other than the one he gave in order to motivate him to live such a colossal lie. But what was it?

1. Could it have been desire for wealth? Religion, we suspect, is yet used for financial gain. However, in this case, all the wealth was on the side of the Jews whom Paul left. Poverty often characterized those with whom he identified. His financial condition as an apostle ranged from providing for himself, and sometimes his co-laborers, by his trade as a tent maker (Acts 18:2-3; 20:33-34; 2 Thessalonians 3:7-8) to receiving wages from some churches to minister to others (2 Corinthians 11:8). But even this did not guarantee that he would always eat (1 Corinthians 4:11). It is not reasonable to further consider lust for money as a motive in Paul's decision to become a Christian. The facts are otherwise.

2. Could it have been a desire for reputation? Personal glorification has ever been a temptation to men of God. What are the facts in this regard? First, he had already received a place of honor among the Jews, having advanced to a place of prominence beyond many of his own age. Second, Saul's name had spread throughout the entire church, prior to his conversion, and beyond. This reputation stood in sharp contrast to his new identity as a member of the sect which was everywhere spoken against (Acts 28:22). As an apostle, he was generally regarded by unbelievers as the scum of the earth (1 Corinthians 4:13). Sometimes he was treated shamefully for preaching the gospel (Acts 14:4-6,19; 17:13-15; 1 Thessalonians 2:1-2). It is unreasonable to charge that Paul changed religions for personal glory. The facts are otherwise.

3. Could it have been a desire for power? He had power with the Jews. And the exercise of his authority as an apostle never gave the slightest hint that he sought power through the Christian religion. The facts are otherwise.

4. *Could it have been a desire for some passion of the flesh?* Divine revelations are known to have been claimed by religious leaders as a pretext to engage in some immoral conduct with sanction. But there is not a blemish of this sort on Paul's record from his youth to his death. Not one of Paul's enemies attempted to put him down by so much as even intimating that his life was morally stained. This was not the reason for his change into Christianity. The facts are otherwise.[43]

5. *Could it have been due to some fear?* Of whom would he have been afraid? As a Jew, he had no one to fear. As a Christian, he feared no one but Christ. The facts are otherwise.

It is conclusive that Paul was sincere when he changed from Judaism. Even granting, for the sake of argument, that Paul did not see the risen Christ, at least it must be admitted that he was absolutely sincere in his conviction that he thought he saw him. Paul was not an imposter. That is conclusive even among critics.

Was Paul Deceived?

His sincerity has been established. But sincere men have been known to be wrong. If wrong, he had to be deceived. But by whom? Christians? How? By what means? Anyway, they could not

43. Taylor Caldwell's fictionalization of a youthful slip into fornication is baseless and totally unnecessary to the presentation of the great life of Paul. "*Great Lion of God.*" Chapter 4.

have when we remember that his conversion came at the height of his fury. Who could have expected to win over his fanaticism? How could they have produced the light that blinded him? The Jews would not have converted their hero away from themselves. The Romans were indifferent to Christianity to begin with. It is unreasonable to suggest that Paul was deceived into thinking he had seen the Lord. No one can be found with the necessary combination of both motive and capability to accomplish the task.

There is yet one other consideration.

Was Paul Mad?

Paul the prisoner was permitted to testify in his own behalf before a lordly assembly including Herod Agrippa and his wife, Bernice, Roman chiliarchs (military officers), and principal men of the city of Caesarea, as well as the governor, Festus, who had arranged the inquiry. At the close of Paul's defense, Festus said loudly, "Paul, thou art mad; thy much learning is turning thee mad" (Acts 26:24). To take Festus' statement at face value is to miss the point. He was certainly not indicting Paul of insanity. He was speaking defensively, for Paul had set forth the resurrection of Jesus in true apologetic style, having presented the evidence in a most skillful and convincing way. Festus attempted to mitigate the power of the apostle's logic by loudly voicing his own judgment of the matter to be ludicrous. But out of the statement, nevertheless, emerges the truth that Paul was quite a capable person far from being a madman.

Agrippa's own evaluation of Paul's defense was quite complimentary. He remarked that "With but little persuasion thou wouldest fain make me a Christian" (Acts 26:28). I do not believe that his statement is to be taken at face value, either. My personal view is that Agrippa's statement was no more than a complimentary expression of admiration and a recognition of Paul's sincerity and obvious apologetic ability which made the story of the resurrection convincingly interesting. If at any moment Agrippa entertained serious thoughts about the credibility of Paul's story, he would not have admitted to it in that assembly. In either case, his diplomatic answer was a testimony to Paul's rationality and logical turn of mind. No one with such ability and decorum could be labeled as a madman. Agrippa's decision would have been to set Paul free had Paul not already appealed for a decision from the emperor (Acts 26:30-32).

Read What He Wrote

Paul's writings are not the product of a deranged mind. They are brilliant literary productions. This is especially clear in the books of Romans and Galatians, which contain superb examples of the logistical ability required to discern and solve the dilemma of how God could be just and at the same time justify lawbreakers. No one who authored such documents could be seriously accused of mental imbalance. In addition to his writings, his sermons, which Luke recorded, bear no faint resemblance to the twisted mentality of madmen. A single reading of his letters and his sermons in the book of Acts will erase any doubt that Paul was anything other than sane, sound, and slightly brilliant.

Summing Up the Modernistic Madness

The fact that Saul of Tarsus did live and did change from persecutor to preacher has been so thoroughly authenticated that the fact is not challenged. But modernists, still unwilling to accept the resurrection, have attempted to explain this historical phenomenon as a psychological cop-out. Saul was supposed to have been so intense in his pursuit of Christians, yet so conscience-stricken for his severe treatment of them, that he became depressed. While on the road to Damascus, he experienced too much heat, which, working on his fevered imagination, caused him merely to think that he saw Jesus! But, as we have already pointed out, this is contrary to the whole historical account of the matter. Precisely here, modernism's prejudice and total disregard for the facts are clearly disclosed. For without the New Testament, we could know nothing of Paul to discuss. It is inconsistent to accept the New Testament account of

Saul of Tarsus, of his life in Judaism, of his conversion, of his characteristic zeal, and then to reject that same account when it offers the resurrection as the cause for his conversion, and then to recommend other causes as possible causes when there is not the first piece of evidence to commend them. To accept the historical accuracy of the New Testament in one place and to reject it without evidence in another exposes a crust of prejudice which no amount of evidence can penetrate.

CONCLUSION

When the evidence from history is arranged and considered objectively, the resurrection becomes believable and the cause for Saul's conversion, otherwise uncertain,[44] receives a logical and satisfying answer.

When ridiculed by Festus, Paul's response, "I am not mad, most excellent Festus; but speak forth words of truth and soberness" (Acts 26:25) was well confirmed by those contemporary events which could easily be checked out by men in high places. As he explained, "this hath not been done in a corner" (Acts 26:26). Paul's life by that time had been

44. Durant, having taken the position that Paul was converted, but not by Jesus Christ, is left with the insoluble riddle of the cause for that conversion. He leaves the matter unsolved and himself wondering: "No one can say what natural processes underlay this pivotal experience." (*Caesar and Christ*, 581.) But the question arises: Is this a fair conclusion from an objective historian when the facts in the case are fully as verifiable as any fact from history?

much publicized. It was more like an open book for all to read. Is it conceivable that Paul perjured himself when to the Galatians he testified to this very matter: "Now touching the things which I write unto you, behold, before God, I lie not." (Galatians 1:20)? Did Paul lie? If Paul was a fake, where lies the fallacy?

9

Jesus in the Context of Miracles

Let me ask you this: If miracles did happen, and those who saw them wanted to tell us about them, how could they have given their report with more authority and credibility than the New Testament writers did?
—Ed Wharton

New Testament writers usually referred to miracles as casually as we refer to a television broadcast. They never made an effort to prove that miracles were performed, they simply referred to them in that take-it-for-granted style which obviated the necessity of proving something that was already common knowledge.

Miracles Were Never Denied

Particularly interesting examples of this lack of denial come from the Jewish opposition. The Jews grudgingly admitted that the miracles were performed; they never once denied their occurrence. When the Pharisees were hard pressed to explain the source of Christ's power to cast out demons, they reasoned defensively that he did so by the power of the prince of demons (Matthew 12:22-24). But in their answer, both demons and Christ's power to cast them out were admitted as facts. John recorded a similar incident when the Jewish leaders became exasperated with Jesus for performing so many signs that multitudes flocked to him. The rulers felt that if Jesus were allowed to continue in such fashion, he would soon bring all Jerusalem to believe on him and that would in turn bring the Romans down on them (John 11:47-53). Their decision, therefore, was to kill him. As far as they were concerned, the miracles were as real as Jesus. Their jealousy prevented them from admitting what the miracles proved. While they denied the deity of Jesus, they never denied that he worked the miracles.

In the third chapter of Acts, Luke records that Peter and John healed a cripple in the temple area. When he began to test his new legs by walking and leaping, he naturally drew a crowd of amazed onlookers who recognized him. The apostles took this as an occasion to preach the gospel and bring more souls to belief in Christ. This provoked the Sadducees to jealousy again, and the authorities promptly arrested them. When they were told to give an account of themselves, Peter responded by pointing to the man whom they had healed and claimed that the healing was done by the power of Jesus of Nazareth whom they had crucified, but whom God had raised from the dead. The force of their words resided in the fact that the former cripple was standing right there in their presence giving credence to everything they said. The Jewish rulers were chagrined. Luke tells us that when they saw the man standing there, they could say nothing against it. We are told that

> *. . . when they had commanded them to go aside out of the council, they conferred among themselves, saying, What shall we do to these men? for that indeed a notable miracle hath been wrought through them, is manifest to all that dwell in Jerusalem; and we cannot deny it. But that it spread no further among the people, let us threaten them, that they speak henceforth to no man in this name.* (Acts 4:15-17)

Rather than attempt to deny the obvious fact of the miracle, the rulers decided to use scare tactics and to threaten the apostles against further preaching. But it never occurred to them to deny the miracles.

When Peter first preached the gospel, he appealed to the miracles of Christ as a confirmation of his claims. It was Pentecost, some fifty-three days since the crucifixion. Thousands of Jews had gathered in Jerusalem from every nation for the great annual feast. With a phenomenal display of wind-sound and a linguistic ability heretofore not exhibited by the apostles—to speak the languages of the nations represented—the multitude of worshippers had their attention drawn keenly toward Peter. He opened his sermon by saying, "Ye men of Israel, hear these words: Jesus of Nazareth, a man approved of God unto you by mighty works and wonders and signs which God did by him in the midst of you, even as ye yourselves know . . . ye by the hand of lawless men did crucify and slay: whom God raised up" (Acts 2:22-24). Their condemnation of Christ was met head-on with the counterclaim that God himself had approved Jesus by the miracles he had performed in their presence. Then, so as not to allow them to escape the force of his evidence, he added, "even as ye yourselves know." As we would say, "He did it, and you know it!" Peter called upon their memories to testify to themselves that Jesus' miracles were proof of God's approval. The miracles were taken for granted. No one ever denied that they happened. The miracles of Christ did not need to be proved; they were the proof to which Peter appealed as confirmation.

Peter's point and mine are the same: If Jesus worked miracles, he is something far more than a mere man. Now the question that comes to my mind is this: How could Peter, among those Jews, expect to get away with such a claim for miracles if they had not happened? Three thousand of those Jews were brought to belief in Jesus as their messiah.

That just would not have happened if they had thought some fanatic was trying to bamboozle them into admitting what thy knew was not true. But the fact is that the church began on that same day with three thousand Jewish converts. What must be answered is: If not miracles, then what forces were present to convince those Jews of the truth of Peter's words?

If Not Miracles, Then What Is Your Alternative?

If you say to yourself that it is difficult to believe that miracles formed the catalyst to bring about belief in Peter's sermon, let me challenge you to produce from a historical basis of facts a reasonable explanation for the three thousand Jews who responded that day. Either these Jews, who had earlier crucified Christ, believed Peter's testimony and endorsed his reference to Jesus' miracles, or they did not. Either Luke's testimony of the establishment of the church on Pentecost was true or it was not true. Did Luke invent the whole story? Tacitus might as well have invented Caesar!

History and Miracles

I want to make two things very clear. First, the miracles of Christ can be verified as factual in the same way that any fact of history can be verified. Second, the miracles of Jesus are a very significant and distinguishing feature of his life and any modern picture of Christ must include this miraculous feature in order to identify with the true Jesus of history.

A Matter of History

When people discuss Christ—not only his existence, but also his personality, teachings, deeds, his relationships with the Jewish community, the dynamic effect he had on others, his death by crucifixion, his burial, and his resurrection—they are admitting that there is a real historical basis for their discussions. Since the New Testament is the only source yielding that information, it is conclusive that the New Testament is that historical basis. Remember that archaeology and first century documentation have confirmed its reliability where they have commented on the same things. What is unintelligent, therefore, about believing the miracles, when this historically reliable testimony says they happened? We can accept them with the same confidence that we accept any other incident to which competent and reliable men testify. Nothing of a historical nature has come to light to discredit them.

What does the evidence say to your reason? Hasn't the New Testament been verified by the same means used on presently accepted histories? What is there of a historical nature that contradicts the New Testament writings? Wouldn't any other document as well verified be considered reliable? Are we not bound to give at least the same consideration to the New Testament that we give to other writings from the same time period? On what basis, then, shall the miracles be rejected? To discount them is to do so at the expense of bonafide evidence and good reason.

Let me ask you this: If the miracles did happen, and those who saw them wanted to tell us about them, how could they have given their report with any more authority and credibility than the New Testament writers did?

A Matter of Consistency

Not even unbelieving historians always discount the miracles as real space-time happenings. Will Durant writes, "That his powers were nevertheless exceptional seems proved by his miracles. . . . The fact that like stories have been told of other characters in legend and history does not prove that the miracles of Christ were myths."[45] We must not make more of Durant's admission of miracles than he intended. He stated that, "With few exceptions they are not beyond belief."[46] But the matter of miracles so generally pervades the entire historical fiber of the gospels and Acts that total disallowance is, at least to Durant, unthinkable.

We must also add that those miracles which Durant would reject are not discounted on any

45. Will Durant, *Caesar and Christ*, pp. 562, 563.
46. Ibid.

grounds of a historical nature. He merely reasons that, "Probably these were in most cases the result of suggestion."[47] However, mere suggestion cannot explain such miracles as raising the dead (Matthew 9:18-25; John 11:43-44) or walking on the water (John 6:16-20). Much less would suggestion allow Jesus to present himself alive after his crucifixion for a personal examination of his pierced hands and side (Luke 24:39-40; John 20:26-29; 1 John 1:1-2). Yet these miracles are a part of the same historical fabric which is admittedly genuine in other places. They can no more be set aside as figments of the writers' imagination than can those miracles which are admitted. There is no less reason of a historical nature to discount these matters than there is to accept the others. Therefore, it becomes a matter of consistency either to accept or reject the entire testimony of the apostles.

Our generation includes a great many people in Europe and Asia and North America who, like Durant, take a cafeteria style approach to the New Testament: they take what they like and discount what they do not like as unbelievable. I have had countless experiences in soul winning with persons who were knowledgeable about the greatness of Jesus and how he has the answers for a corrupt world, but clearly conveyed that they "do not believe in all those miracles." In answer, please consider why anyone would believe that Jesus did

47. Ibid.

anything at all. The answer is always the same—because the New Testament says so. Do not forget that outside that New Testament, we can know nothing of the life and teachings of Christ, only that he lived and died at Jerusalem. If we say that Jesus did anything at all, we are saying that the New Testament is reliable, at least at that point. If we admit that Jesus worked any miracles at all, just one miracle, we admit that the New Testament is telling us the truth about that particular matter. But why have we admitted the truth of the testimony at that point? Has there been an investigation into its genuineness? Has there been an evaluation of the evidence and a reasonable conclusion reached consistent with the evidence? In answer to this, would we only shrug our shoulders? Or would we candidly admit that those scholastic investigations have been made by others and that we feel safe to agree with the general consensus?

Now consider why anyone would not believe the miracles. Is it because there is a genuine ground of historical evidence that throws reasonable doubt on them? We know that this is not the real reason for dismissing the miracles. The real reason is prejudice. There exists a presupposition that some miracles, or all of them, could not have happened in the natural world, and, therefore, the New Testament account of them is wrong, even though the evidence is difficult to deny.

This is not the way that history testifies to any event. Historical truth can neither be confirmed nor refuted by a presupposition that some particular thing could or could not have happened. This is no way to treat perfectly good historical testimony to any kind of claim. What justification is there for treating the historic Christian Scriptures with such a groundless and haughty glibness? If modern men will consistently apply the historical method to the miracles, their eyes will be opened to the inequalities of religious liberals when they reject the historical basis of Christianity strictly at the point of miracles, while at the same time, they accept it elsewhere.

Jesus and Miracles

The gospel writers wrote their papers to prove to us that Jesus is the son of God. They set about to accomplish their task by pointing us toward the miracles he did in their presence (John 20:30-31). The miraculous element is presented in such quantity that the picture of Jesus which emerges from those pages virtually immerses him in a life-context of miracles.

Modern Theology's Jesus of History

The modern portrait of Jesus is strictly human. The miracle stories are debunked as being out of character with the rest of Christ's life, supposedly giving us a distorted picture of the real Jesus. This is due to modern theology which has it that the real Jesus lies hidden beneath a gospel-myth. The church is supposed to be the culprit, having heroized him so that as his story was told and retold, there developed a supernaturalism about him. Supernatural claims and deeds were attributed to him over a period of thirty years so that by the time Mark wrote his gospel, the legend was supposed to be confused with history.

Jesus Christ, Superstar!

This is illustrated in the modern opera, *Jesus Christ, Superstar*. It begins with Judas saying,

> If you strip away the myth from the man
> You will see where we all soon will be
> Jesus! You've started to believe
> The things they say of you
> You really do believe
> This talk of God is true.

Superstar's message is clear: Jesus was a man like any modern man we see today, and when we strip away the myth from the gospel, we will see him as he really was. Modern theology tells today's man that if we de-mythologize the New Testament—take away the miracles—we will get back to the real Jesus of history.

But where is the evidence that the miracles are mythical? It does not exist. Merely saying the miracles are myth is not proof. They are embedded in the context of a totally reliable testimony. The whole matter of myth-miracles is assumed on the basis of a presupposition that miracles could not have happened, reliable historical testimony to the contrary notwithstanding.

Take a Serious Look at the Facts

Modernism contradicts the indisputable fact that the church was established in Jerusalem just fifty days after the crucifixion; it was established on the major belief that Jesus had been resurrected from the dead. It did not take thirty years for a supernatural Jesus to become identified with Christianity. In only fifty days from his journey to the cross, his bodily resurrection became the foundation stone upon which thousands, including many who had participated in condemning him, confessed their faith in him as Lord and were ushered into the church. Fifty days is not enough time to develop a myth about a miracle-working Christ who had been raised from the dead and then pass it off on thousands of Jews who knew better!

Coming to Grips With the Facts

Let's face it: the church began with a belief in the supernatural Jesus. Then in the days to come, that faith empowered the church to maintain its hope and growth momentum through severe hardship. If miracles were not a real part of the historical Jesus, then what alternative reason can be offered for the dynamic conviction which moved thousands of Jews to accept Jesus as their Lord and stay with him faithfully to the death?

"De-Mything" the Modern Myth

The real mythology is that the "real" Jesus of modernism has something to offer twentieth century man. We are not allowed to believe that he made a single claim to deity or that he worked a single miracle. What was it the modern Jesus Christ said or did that was so outstanding beyond any other modern man?

You will search the New Testament endlessly to find an outstanding statement or claim or deed done by Jesus which is not connected directly or contextually to his divine nature, his messiahship, or his mission as Saviour of the world. What would the modern Jesus have to offer anyone? If the so-called de-mythologization is carried out—which means that all miracles and supernatural and messianic claims are to be thrown out—the Jesus who would be left would be lifeless and speechless. He would be without meaning either to the people of his day or of ours. Try it and see. It's unreasonable that the "modern Jesus" could have produced such a stir in the ancient world, such conviction in the hearts of so many, such a powerful and lasting ethic, such a hope for eternal redemption, and to have done it all without having said or done anything outstanding!

The Miracles of Jesus Are "In Character"

"In character" means that the miracles of Christ are in keeping with the general life and character of Jesus as presented to us in the gospel accounts. The general picture of Jesus is such that miracles are not at all out of place in this particular portrait. Consider the following attributes, claims, and deeds which are a part of the picture of Jesus that emerges from the New Testament.

1. His virgin birth (Matthew 1:18-23; Luke 1:26-35).
2. His boyhood wisdom exemplified in his penetrating understanding and concept of the law at the youthful age of twelve (Luke 2:40-52).
3. His uncanny perception into the heart, motives, and thoughts of others (John 1:47-48; 2:24-25; 4:16-19; 6:15, 61, 70; 13:1-3, 21-30).
4. His foretelling of future events:
   a. The betrayal by Judas (Matthew 26:20-21; Luke 22:21-22; John 13:21-27).
   b. Peter's denial (Matthew 26:34; Mark 14:30; John 13:38).
   c. The destruction of Jerusalem wherein Jesus foretold the coming of the Roman legions and their encircling of the city (Matthew 23: 29-24:34; Mark 13:1-32; Luke 19:41-44; 21: 5-33).
   d. His own death and the manner of it (Matthew 16:21; 17:22-23; 20:19; John 2:19-21; 12:32-33), though they attempted to kill him by other means (John 5:18; 7:1; 8:59; 10:31, 39).

5. His claims are those of a liar and a blasphemer *or* those of the son of God, for he claimed:
   a. That he would build his church and that death could not stop him (Matthew 16:13-19).
   b. To be the Messiah of Old Testament prophecy (Luke 4:16-21; 24:25-27, 44-47; John 4:25-26; 5:39).
   c. To be able to forgive sins (Matthew 9:2; Mark 2:5; Luke 19:10).
   d. To be the son of God (Matthew 16:13-20; John 5:19-26; 10:36).
   e. That his origin and nature were different from others (John 8:23-24).
   f. That he had existence before Abraham (John 8:58).
   g. That he will open the tombs of all men and raise the dead to judgment (John 5:28-29).
   h. That no one can come to God except through him (John 14:6), thus excluding all others as mediators between God and man.
   i. That his words will judge us (John 12:48-50).
   j. That he was sinless and able to free us from the bondage of sin (John 8:29, 34-36, 46).
   k. That he would send the Holy Spirit from heaven to the apostles in order to guide them into a remembrance of all he said while on earth, and into a full knowledge of the meaning of the gospel (John

14:16-18, 26; 16:7, 13-14).

l. That he is the resurrection and the life (John 11:25).

m. That he will come again to receive us to be with him where he is (John 14:3). These claims circumscribe the attributes of divine nature, divine power, and divine right—in short, all the divine attributes of God himself. In what way would the miracles attributed to Christ be out of character with the one who made such claims? Obviously, the miracles are no more outstanding to the general picture of Christ than are his claims.

6. His moral glory. There is a perfect integration between the ideal man back of his claims and the life he lived in perfect harmony with those claims. No flaw can be detected in the picture of his life as we have it.
7. His authority and wisdom. Matthew's record of the Sermon on the Mount, chapters 5-7. Other instances (Matthew 13:54; 22:23-46 where he put his challengers to silence. Also Mark 6:2; 11:18; Luke 4:32). Whence came this wisdom? Even the Jewish opposition acknowledged his intellectual powers and admitted an inability to account for it (John 7:14-16).
8. His death by crucifixion was accomplished in six hours! (Mark 15:33-37, 43-45). Usually the executed would hang on the cross for two

to three days, sometimes for a week, before finally expiring. This is a very significant point when we consider that Jesus claimed to have power over his own life so that no one could take his life from him (John 10:17-18; 14:30-31). (This point will be fully developed in the next chapter.)

9. His resurrection as presented in the four gospels.
10. His ascension in the clouds of heaven in the sight of the apostles (Acts 1:9-11).

The life of Jesus as presented in the gospels is one of supernatural events and divine claims. Jesus lived in the context of miracles. The miracles are not out of character with the general picture of Jesus which the gospel writers have given us. To the contrary, the miracles attributed to him are no more outstanding than are his divine claims, his virgin birth, his sinless life, his prophetic ability, his profound wisdom, or his unique death on the cross in only six hours.

H. G. Wells has written: "We shall tell what men believed about Jesus of Nazareth, but him we shall treat as being what he appeared to be, a man, just as a painter must needs paint him as a man."[48] However, in the light of the picture of Christ which the gospel writers have painted, I feel constrained to ask at what point in that gospel portrait does

48. H. G. Wells, *The Outline of History*, Vol. 1, p. 420.

Jesus ever appear to be merely a man? From his birth to his death, at all points in between and beyond the grave, the literary picture of Jesus Christ is distinctly that of a divine person, not merely that of a man.

Conclusion

Jesus himself calls us to believe in him on the ground of his miraculous works (John 10:37-38). John affirms that he heard Jesus say this, and that he was an eyewitness of those "works of God" (John 19:35; 20:30-31). Since the Gospel records are historically reliable, and the miracles of Christ which are presented in them are generally in character with the rest of the life of Christ, it is reasonable to conclude that the miracles of Jesus Christ are as authentic as the very life of Jesus Christ himself and that he is therefore the son of God.

10

Jesus: the Man of Destiny

We have reason to expect that an ordinary man would have survived the ordeal of crucifixion had he been removed from the cross after only six hours. But, remarkably, Jesus, after only six hours on the cross, announced with a strong voice that this was the very moment of his death, and immediately he died!

The Destiny of Death

One of the most remarkable aspects of the historical Jesus was the power of control which he exercised over his own life, as well as the entire society of Palestinian Jews, in order to bring about his death by crucifixion. The extraordinary quality of this unusual phenomenon is highlighted by the following facts: Jesus stayed alive and at liberty while circulating among the Jews who were attempting to arrest and kill him, his death by crucifixion was in fulfillment of his claims that he would die in that particular manner and in spite of earlier Jewish efforts to kill him by other means, and the time that he spent dying on the cross was much shorter than the killing time normally required by crucifixion. When ordinary men are placed in these same circumstances, we expect to see them lose control. Amazingly, Jesus controlled the direction of his life and the manner of his death in fulfillment of his claims.

Such power can only reasonably be attributed to God. Therefore, these historical facts form a strong and reasonable case for believing that Jesus possessed the power of God and that he was here in fulfillment of a certain divine destiny.

Examine the Claims

Jesus Claimed That He Would Die by Crucifixion

Throughout his life, there were a number of attempts to kill him by means other than the cross, but they all failed. The reason which both Jesus and John assigned to these unsuccessful attempts was that Jesus' "hour had not yet come" (John 7:6, 8, 30; 8:20). To Jesus, this "hour" was evidently a predetermined assignment for the future which he had been sent to fulfill. Later he explained that this particular moment was the hour of his death, "The hour is come, that the Son of man should be glorified. Verily, verily, I say unto you, Except a grain of wheat fall into the earth and die, it abideth by itself alone; but if it die, it beareth much fruit. He that loveth his life loseth it. . . . Now is my soul troubled; and what shall I say? Father, save me from this hour. But for this cause came I unto this hour" (John 12:23-27). On the eve of his crucifixion, he told his disciples clearly that the hour of his destiny was the hour of his death. John prefaced the going forth of Judas to betray Christ with the statement that Jesus knew that his hour had come to depart out of this world unto the Father (John 13:1). Such a departure could only mean death. But Jesus was careful to point out that the manner of that death was to be a crucifixion. Matthew records that "he took the twelve disciples apart, and on the way he said unto them, Behold we go up to Jerusalem; and the Son of man shall be delivered unto the chief priests and scribes; and they shall condemn him to death, and shall deliver him unto the Gentiles to mock, and to scourge, and to crucify" (Matthew 20:17-19). He said to Nicodemus, "As Moses lifted up the serpent in the wilderness, even so must the Son of man be lifted up" (John 3:14). At the moment when he declared that his "hour" was imminent, he assigned that he would be "lifted up" on a cross: "And I, if I be lifted up from the earth, will draw all men unto myself. But this he said, signifying by what manner of death he should die" (John 12:32-33).

It is conclusive that Jesus viewed his death upon a cross to be an unalterable part of the divine destiny.

Jesus Claimed to Have the Power of Divine Providence

Jesus stated in John 10:17-18, "Therefore doth the Father love me, because I lay down my life, that I may take it again. No one taketh it away from me, but I lay it down of myself. I have power to lay it down, and I have power to take it again."

Few words, even in the Bible, lay claim to so broad a compass. These words actually embrace the concept of divine providence, which is that prerogative of God when he exercises his sovereign power to overrule and to interfere in the historical framework of men and nations to bring to pass his own desired goals. Inherent in Jesus' statement that no one could take his life from him is his claim to that kind of power. It was another way of saying that he was in control of those circumstances which touched both his own life and those of his enemies who were seeking a way and an opportunity to kill him.

Jesus came to die, and the Jewish leaders wanted him dead. But the battle at this point between them was the time and manner of death that Jesus wanted versus the time and manner of death the Jews wanted. Jesus came to die only by crucifixion and at the fixed place (outside of the city of

Jerusalem, Hebrews 13:11-13) and at the fixed time, which the Father had predestined. The Jewish powers, on the other hand, were seeking *any* opportunity to rid themselves of their tormentor which they could manage without creating an uproar against them from the multitudes of the common people. It was in the heat of this conflict, when both sides were taking measures and counter-measures, that Jesus claimed that he had the power to keep anyone from taking his life. He had a certain destiny to fulfill and no power from hell or on earth could alter it.

When Jesus was taken before Pilate, the Roman procurator, unable to prod him as some ordinary criminal into the kind of fearful response he thought his official dignity required, in exasperation said, "Speakest thou not unto me? knowest thou not that I have power to release thee, and have power to crucify thee?" But Jesus replied, "Thou wouldest have no power against me, except it were given thee from above" (John 19:10-11). As far as Jesus was concerned, there was no power against him which could effect a change in the course of his divine destiny. Therefore, Pilate's decision to crucify him was less his own doing than God's. It was Christ's decision to accept the death at Golgotha as a part of his own prearranged plan. Pilate, Jesus claimed, was but an unwitting part of the plan.

Jesus Was Not a Victim of Circumstances

In this view of the forces which combined to bring about the death of Christ, we cannot accept the nonhistorical view of *Jesus Christ, Superstar*, which makes him out to be a victim of circumstances which he could not control. According to the historical accounts of Jesus' claims and the outcome of the whole matter as confirmed in the resurrection, Jesus himself was in control of every circumstance during every step of the way. Later, the apostle Paul would write that Jesus, the incarnate God, in obedience to the Father's eternal purpose, humbled himself to die on the cross (Philippians 2:5-8). He was not a victim of circumstances beyond his control, nor was he humbled by superior powers which finally succeeded in killing him. To the contrary, he controlled the direction of his life, in the midst of opposing forces, as to the time and place of his own choosing and humbled himself to the deadly desires of the ruling Jews, laying down his own life, on schedule, according to plan.

Jesus Claimed That He Had Power to Lay Down His Life

Examine his statement closely. He said, "*I lay down my life*, that I may take it again. No one taketh it away from me, but *I lay it down of myself. I have power to lay it down*, and I have power to take it again." This is distinct from his claim to have power to keep his life and to choose the manner of his death. In this instance, Jesus claimed the ability to die at any given moment, to give up his life's breath at any time he wished. As we will see, this power would have been highly desirable to anyone who had been unfortunately sentenced to suffer the inhuman torture of death by crucifixion.

These claims and the power to accomplish them, as already mentioned, can reasonably be attributed only to God. The proposition of the New Testament writers is that Jesus made good on those claims and that their accounts accurately record the facts in the case which bear them out.

Examine the Facts

The claims for Christ having been made, we turn now to a consideration of those facts touching his life and death which will reflect the truth or falsity of those claims.

No One Could Kill Him

From infancy, Jesus was under the threat of death. When Herod the Great, true to his murderous character, heard that Jesus was born to the messianic throne of David, he ordered the death of all the male children in and around Bethlehem up to two years old. But Joseph and Mary took Jesus and scurried to Egypt when they were forewarned of Herod's intentions (Matthew 2). At the outset of his ministry, his messianic claims infuriated the members of the synagogue at Nazareth, who thereupon, Luke informs us, "cast him forth out of the city, and led him unto the brow of the hill whereon their city was built, that they might throw him down headlong. But he passing through the midst of them went his way" (Luke 4:28-30). Luke does not attempt to explain Jesus' escape method; he only recorded the fact that Jesus passed through their midst and went his way (not "away," but "his way," indicating his own chosen way as opposed to theirs). This is commensurate with the Lord's claims to have the power of divine providence and the consequent inability of another to take his life from him.

At one point in his ministry, officers were sent from the ruling Jews to arrest him. Even this effort was aborted. The officers returned and testified as to the reason for their failure to carry out their commission: "Never man so spake!" (John 7:32, 45-46). The impact of the doctrine of Christ was often said to be astonishing (Matthew 7:28; Mark 1:22; 6:2; Luke 4:32, etc.). Inherent in the answer of the officers is a confirmation of that claim.

Any number of attempts to kill Jesus by stoning also failed (John 8:59; 10:31, 39). His entire public ministry was threatened by attempts to kill him one way or another (Matthew 12:14; John 5:18; 7:1,19, 25; 8:37, 40; 11:47-53), yet they all failed. Be cautious about comparing Jesus with today's criminal who eludes the efforts of law enforcement agencies until finally he is caught. The criminal is on the run, hiding, making every effort to stay away from those pursuing him. But, to the contrary, Jesus walked openly in their midst and taught publicly in their temple and attended the feasts. This caused the multitudes of the people who observed these things a bit of consternation. They wondered about it and John reported that "Some therefore of them of Jerusalem said, Is not this he whom they seek to kill? And lo, he speaketh openly, and they say nothing unto him. Can it be that the rulers indeed know that this is the Christ?" (John 7:25-26).

The futility of their attempts upon his life, for whatever reasons may be supposed, nevertheless, confirmed his claim to have power over his life and over theirs to the extent that they could not kill him though they tried.

Jesus Died Voluntarily

The fact that Jesus died of his own volition and at the very moment of his own choosing, not by the effects of the crucifixion, has not received the attention that it warrants. Yet this amazing fact has been stated clearly enough by all four of the gospel historians. Perhaps this is because crucifixion, as a means of execution, is so far removed from our modern frame of reference that none of the effects or requirements upon the one being crucified are generally known. That is very possibly why the unique circumstances accompanying the death of Jesus on the cross are not recognized, even by the great mass of Bible readers. If this is the situation, then, the following few considerations should be far in excess of mere academic interest, especially since the death of the historical Jesus, as set out in the New Testament, has never been seriously challenged.

Killing Time on a Cross

The death of the crucified victim was brought about either by starvation or by exhaustion, but not by loss of blood. If he was tied to the cross, nothing more was done and he was left to starve to death.[49] If he was nailed to the cross, an improvised saddle of wood was made for him to rest his body on to prevent his wounds from tearing apart as his body sagged from exhaustion. This may have produced some insignificant bleeding, but not fatally so. Death rarely resulted before a day and a half to three days, depending entirely on the constitution of the individual.

This explains why the Jews broke the legs of the thieves who were crucified on either side of Jesus. The day following the crucifixion was a Sabbath day, and the Jews wanted the victims taken away prior to that time; thus, their legs were broken to accelerate their deaths by preventing them from supporting their bodies in order to breathe (John 19:31-33).

49. *International Standard Bible Encyclopaedia*, Vol. 11, pp. 761-762.

Jesus Died in Six Hours!

Mark tells us that Jesus was crucified at the third hour,[50] about nine o'clock in the morning, and that he died at the ninth hour, about three o'clock in the afternoon (Mark 15:25-37). The importance of this fact cannot be overstated. Had Jesus remained alive on the cross for the length of time it ordinarily took to die by crucifixion, there would have been no evidence that he had exercised his divine power to lay down his life by an act of his own will as he had earlier claimed. It would have appeared that he had died like any other man on a cross. It was therefore necessary for death to ensue early, while yet the strength of life was surging through his body. We have reason to expect that an ordinary man would have survived the ordeal of crucifixion had he been removed from the cross after only six hours. But, remarkably, Jesus, after only six hours on the cross, announced with a strong voice that this was the very moment of his death, and immediately he died! (Luke 23:46; John 19:30).

This explains Pilate's surprise when slightly more than six hours had lapsed before Joseph of

50. The alleged contradiction between Mark's record of the time of the crucifixion and John's is without merit. John's statement that it was the sixth hour when they led Jesus out to be crucified (19:14-16) is accomodating Gentiles to whom he wrote his book. The Jews' counted time from 6 PM to 6 AM. The Gentiles counted time as we do from 12 AM to 12 PM. Thus John is in perfect agreement with Mark.

Arimathaea requested of the governor that the body of Jesus be given to him. Mark says that "Pilate marvelled if he were already dead," and called for the centurion of the execution squad to confirm the Lord's death (Mark 15:43-45). Pilate marvelled inasmuch as it was too soon for the normal expectation of death by crucifixion.

Jesus Died Voluntarily!

It is stated with clarity in all four of the Gospel accounts that Jesus died by an effort of his own will. Matthew states that "Jesus cried again with a loud voice, and yielded up his spirit" (Matthew 27:50). Mark said, "And Jesus uttered a loud voice, and gave up the ghost" (Mark 15:37). Luke has it that, "Jesus, crying with a loud voice, said, Father, into thy hands I commend my spirit: and having said this, he gave up the ghost" (Luke 23:46). And John wrote, "he said, It is finished: and he bowed his head, and gave up his spirit" (John 19:30). Luke refers to Christ's death as an accomplishment (Luke 9:31).

The death of Jesus was the result of giving up his life-spirit. His loud proclamation just before death proves that he had much physical strength yet in him. There is no indication that he was any where near death at that time. His life did not ebb away; it was voluntarily given away while he was still very strong physically. He did not pale away into unconsciousness, nor did he go into a coma. He was not exhausted, as were ordinary men who had fought the cross for thirty-six to seventy-two hours. He simply reached the point in time when he decided to die. He pronounced his work finished, commended his spirit to the Father, bowed his head (showing his head to be upright to this point and his physical strength still within him), and immediately gave up his life-spirit. He died by an act of his will at the precise moment of his own choosing.

Paid in Full

In the Koine Greek, the language in which the New Testament was written, the words "It is finished" is only one word, *tetelestai*. That word means that a debt has been paid in full. When this meaning is placed together with the claims of Christ to give his life a ransom for us (Matthew 20:28) that we might have eternal life and with the fact that he died immediately after saying, "It is finished," a harmony of his doctrine and death is revealed which can hardly be explained as coincidental. He claimed he would give his life to buy us back from the death penalty. Then he died immediately after saying that the penalty had been paid in full! The doctrine of his death and the fact that his death followed immediately after his claim that his work was finished—that he had paid the ransom—could not have been mere happenstance: too many things had to transpire harmoniously in one brief moment of time.

The Roman Centurion Was Made a Believer

The entire matter of Jesus' death was contrary to the agony of death by crucifixion, which they had naturally expected. How could he have died with his strength still in him? How could he possibly have known the moment of his death if he were only human? The fact is he did. For this reason, the centurion who "saw that he *so* gave up the ghost . . . said, Truly this man was the son of God" (Mark 15:39), and glorified God further by saying, "Certainly this was a righteous man" (Luke 23:47). The centurion, could see that Jesus' death was not at all like any crucifixion he had ever witnessed or knew anything about. Matthew refers to all these things that were done and offers them as the reason for the centurion's great fear (Matthew 27:54).

The question is: Can we expect a mere man to have the kind of power and control over his own life and the lives of many others, as Jesus apparently did, especially when opposed by the power and intention of the ruling Jews to force him another direction? Whence came the power that Jesus had to preserve his life against what we would consider to be superior forces and overwhelming odds? Can we reasonably expect a mere human being to be able to give up his life after only six hours on a cross, contrary to the nature of slow death by crucifixion? Certainly not. How, then, could we possibly explain the entire matter of Jesus' life in the face of death, his claim to die a particular death for a particular reason, and the fact of his death at the very moment he spoke it, if he were no more than human?

Conclusion

The facts surrounding the life and death of Jesus and his claims in regard to that life and death are such that they lend great credibility to his claim to be the son of God. Attempts to either capture or kill him prior to the time of his choosing were defeated one after the other. His death on the cross was too soon to be expected of the normal procedure. His death by crucifixion, not another means of death, fulfilled his claims to die in that particular manner. All of this, plus his confidence throughout his life to the moment he died that he would accomplish his purpose as he foretold it, should be sufficient to convince an honest person of this century that Jesus Christ was in control both of his life and the lives and circumstances of all those that were about him.

On the basis of these facts, it is reasonable to believe that Jesus of Nazareth is the son of God, that he came to us on a mission of redemption according to the Father's foreordained plan, that Jesus was a man of a certain destiny, and that he fulfilled it at the cross.

First Appendix

The Value of the Critical View of the New Testament

11

The Value of the Critical View of the New Testament

> *From within the biblical tradition we must insist and confidently expect that the more profoundly and validly we understand and interpret the Bible, the greater the religious depth with which it will challenge and speak to us. It is precisely here that modern biblical scholarship has proved itself so insipid and unstimulating.*
>
> —J. V. Langmead Casserley

Christianity is a historical religion. It is not to be viewed as merely ethical or moral, consisting simply of rules and regulations. Jesus came to provide redemption from sin and death by means of his life, death, and resurrection. That redemption is only as real as those events. It is necessary to view the New Testament as a record of the genuine historicity of those events if Christianity is to become a dynamic sufficient to change lives and to create a genuine hope for a future life.

The following quotations will help explain the importance of viewing the Scriptures as historically trustworthy. Edward J. Young, the late Protestant scholar, has written:

> When, however, we come to examine the question what we are to believe we discover that the doctrines which Scripture commends are rooted and grounded upon that which was done in history. The Christian faith, as it is revealed in the Bible, is not a mass of abstractions divorced from history. It is not eternal truths and ideals, but rather the account of something that God did for us upon this earth in history. Hence, it becomes very important to us to know whether what the Bible has to say about these historical matters is correct or not.
>
> According to the Bible our salvation depends upon the death of Jesus Christ at Calvary and upon his subsequent resurrection from the dead. Now, it is quite important to know certain details about the tomb in which He was laid. Was that tomb empty upon the third day? Was there an actual historical resurrection or not? Questions such as these intrude themselves into our consideration and will not be pushed aside. Is the Bible, therefore, correct in what it has to say of these historical details or not? If the historical framework in which the great redemptive acts of God took place is a frame-

> work which is not to be trusted, how do we know that we have a true and correct account of those redemptive acts themselves?[51]

In other words, history and faith cannot be divorced without destroying the real power of Christianity. To remove faith from its historical base is to remove Christ from his power to save from sin and to raise the dead. F. F. Bruce explains it this way:

> For the Christian gospel is not primarily a code of ethics or a metaphysical system; it is first and foremost good news, and as such it was proclaimed by its earliest preachers. . . . And this good news is intimately bound up with the historical order, for it tells how for the world's redemption God entered into history, the eternal came into time, the kingdom of heaven invaded the realm of earth, in the great events of the incarnation, crucifixion, and resurrection of Jesus the Christ. The first recorded words of our Lord's public preaching in Galilee are: "The time is fulfilled, and the kingdom of God has drawn near; repent and believe the good news."[52]

The good news which Christ announced was that God's own kingdom was about to be established, and he asked men to believe it. He also

51. Edward J. Young, *Thy Word Is Truth*, pp. 100-101.
52. F. F. Bruce, *The New Testament Documents*, pp. 7, 8.

announced that the kingdom would be established with power during the lifetime of that generation of people (Mark 9:1). Then he demonstrated that power in his own bodily resurrection. It was by faith in that historic event that men believed in the good news of that kingdom and were baptized into it (Acts 8:12; Colossians 1:13-14). If we separate faith from that historical resurrection, there would be no good news concerning the kingdom of God, and Christianity could be nothing more than an idealistic sentiment. Either the New Testament relates to us the factual truth of Jesus Christ's divine power in his miracles and resurrection, or, if it is not historic fact, there is no hope for the human race beyond the grave.

The Critical View of Scripture

Due to the great volume of liberal literature and an appreciable degree of success to equate higher criticism with true Bible scholarship, coupled with the fact that this generation has generally accepted evolution as the great life principle, many are now questioning the relevance of the Scriptures to their lives. When this is taken together with another fact, that the Bible is constantly being thrust into a liberal interpretation, not only in literature, but from the lowest to the highest levels of classroom instruction, and more increasingly by the film media, it should appear essential for the Christian, from the least to the greatest, to know something of the real nature of this modern approach to the Bible.

There are two very good reasons for investigating the nature of criticism. First, in order to see that the critical view has no real genuine value as a means of determining biblical truth, and second, to enable the Christian to distinguish between true Bible exposition and plain unbelief in the guise of religious scholarship.

Liberalism Rejects the Historical Reliability of the Gospels

Christians should not be naive to the fact that not all who deal with the Bible believe it to be historically reliable. Many so-called theologians speak of their belief in Christ and even express their appreciation for his ethical teachings but will make it clear that they do not believe that they are set in a truly historical framework. They insist that the gospel miracles, such as the virgin birth and the resurrection, are not factual, but that they detract from the true picture of the historical Jesus.

1. Liberalism recommends a de-mythologizing of the gospels.

Liberalism's rejection of the historical trustworthiness of the gospels is manifested in the glib recommendation, which most university students have heard, that the gospels should be de-mythologized. Back of this approach to the Scriptures lies the debunking efforts of men like Karl Barth, Soren Kierkegaard, and Rudolph Bultmann who taught that the facts of history are not necessary to have faith in Christ, and that the gospels, the apostles' teaching about the supernatural Christ and the kingdom of God, are all mythology.[53]

This de-mythologization is illustrated in the modern claim that the church over a period of some thirty years exaggerated the truth about Jesus and developed a supernatural, bodily resurrected Christ and attributed to him divine claims and miracles for which he himself was not responsible. By the time the first gospel was written (about A.D. 60-62) Mark was not supposed to know the difference between the mythical Jesus and the real Jesus. Apparently, it does not bother the critic at all that there is no evidence for this claim. This so-called church-produced myth is purely the result of conjecture, nothing more, which is based upon the presupposition that miracles could not have happened. The fact that there is evidence in the gospels of a totally historical and verifiable sort that miracles and the resurrection did take place is of no consequence to the critic. He still clings to his bias against miracles and sets about to debunk the gospels as historically unreliable. Furthermore, the critic seems completely oblivious to the fact that

53. Rudolph Bultmann, *Theology of the New Testament*, Vol. 11, will illustrate this.

the historic church was established just fifty days after the crucifixion on the belief that Jesus was the resurrected son of God. It should be evident that fifty days is hardly enough time to develop a legend around a person who had so recently been in their midst.

It is amazing that any Bible student would seriously consider the modern view, based as it is on mere conjecture without evidence and in total disregard for the historical evidence available to us. Edward J. Young evaluated the liberal approach by indicting it of having erected a man of straw to fight.[54] That evaluation seems very accurate.

2. Liberalism assumes that the gospels are theology and therefore not history.

Charles Augustus Briggs, of a past generation but of the critical persuasion, says of his view of the Bible's infallibility in relation to faith and practice:

> They [the Scriptures] are infallible in all matters of divine revelation, in all things where men need infallible guidance from God. We do not thereby claim that a writer dwelling in Palestine had an infallible knowledge of countries he had never visited, of dates of events beyond his own experience where he had to rely upon tradition or doubtful or imperfect human records. We do not affirm that he gave an exact and infalli-

54. Edward J. Young, *Thy Word Is Truth*, p. 15.

> ble report of words spoken centuries before, which had never before been previously recorded; or an infallible description of events that happened in distant lands and ages. . . . We do not thereby claim that the writer of the poem of the creation knew geology and astronomy, and natural history better than the experts of modern science, but to teach us the science of God and redemption, and the art of living holy, godlike, lives the Bible is the only infallible rule of faith and practice.[55]

The idea that the Bible is the infallible rule of faith and practice but cannot be completely relied on or believed is an inconsistency which most persons would reject. But not the critic; he does not believe that the Bible has to tell the truth to be worthy of producing an infallible faith!

Leon Morris, a Bible believer himself, presents the critic's view of the historicity of the gospel of John in the following words,

> But because he (John) is a theologian and undoubtedly presents theology in this book, questions arise: What are we supposed to make of the incidents he relates? Are these meant to be stories of things that actually occurred? Or is he simply manufacturing incidents (as the Master composed parables) that will serve his purpose of edification?

55. *The Bible, the Church, and the Reason,* pp. 93-94.

> Perhaps he is taking a basis of fact and erecting upon it a superstructure which, while sound theologically, is questionable when it comes to matters of historical fact.[56]

What this amounts to is clearly stated by the critic himself, that the gospels are "questionable when it comes to matters of historical fact." But, as he says, that is supposed to be all right as long as the structure is "sound theologically." And if we are worried that this kind of a theological structure is shaky since it is erected upon events that did not actually take place, the critic quickly justifies it on the basis that even "the Master composed parables."

However, this approach is tragically wrong on at least two counts. First, consider how we know that "the Master composed parables." Is it not because the gospel writers said that he did? Therefore, the critic has admitted that the gospels contain some events which did happen which are clearly historical in nature. So, according to the modern view, it is a matter of historical truth that the Master composed parables. But if the modern view is right, that in matters of historical fact the gospels are questionable, then even here the matter of the Master composing parables is also questionable!

The critical view at best is theological doubletalk. In the final analysis, the modern view is

56. Leon Morris, *Studies in the Fourth Gospel,* p. 65.

illogical and self-contradictory. By applying its own methods to itself it can be seen that nothing in the Bible could be known to have happened, thus abolishing any solid basis upon which to construct any kind of theology.

Second, consider the plain, unveiled statements of the gospel writers that they earnestly desire for us to receive what they wrote as matters of historical fact. Luke's literary works (Luke and Acts) are the result of careful research and an accurate accounting of the historic events that transpired during the very time in which he and his correspondent, Theophilus, lived. He makes a plain statement that the purpose of such precision in research and writing was that Theophilus might "know the certainty concerning the things" about which he had been taught (Luke 1:1-4). John recorded the messianic and divine claims which Jesus made for himself, the miraculous signs which Jesus performed, and Jesus' own appeal to the signs as proof that he and God are one (John 10:37-38). Then, as if to answer the critic of today, John said that his testimony is true and that the reason for writing his gospel was that we may believe in the risen Lord (John 19:35; 20:30-31). According to the gospels, saving faith is located in the historically crucified and risen Jesus. The only thing left for the reader of the gospels to deduct is whether the historical evidence sustains the divine claims.

The whole point of the gospel testimony is that God acted through Jesus in history that men might make a certain judgment for their eternal welfare (John 9:39). And that action took place in a sequence of events which can be located at specific times and places.

3. Liberalism conjectures that the gospel writers invented the speeches of Jesus.

It is not difficult to find liberal writings which tell us that men of antiquity composed fictional stories and speeches for their heroes in order to bring out ethical truth. Morris explains that those who take such positions make little effort to prove them.

> They assert that in antiquity this was a recognized and respected procedure. If we wanted to bring out the truth about Jesus, they might say, we would distinguish carefully between, for example, what Jesus said and what we deduce from his words. But in the first century a man would regard it as perfectly acceptable, for example, if he were quite convinced that Jesus thought of himself as the Messiah, to report that Jesus had claimed this. Thus, we must expect that John would compose "sayings" of Jesus, and manufacture incidents in which Jesus' character and claims are made plain.[57]

57. Morris, *Studies in the Fourth Gospel*, p. 68.

An example of this very thing is illustrated in Hugh J. Schoenfield's, *The Passover Plot*,

> But also we cannot ignore that in the interests of theological doctrine, contemporary circumstances, and effective storytelling, nothing wrong was seen in creating views for Jesus to express, altering the sense of traditional sayings of his, supplying and colouring episodes with the help of non-Christian literature.[58]

In other words, liberalism asserts that the speeches recorded by the gospel writers which are attributed to Jesus cannot really be trusted to have come from the lips of Jesus, but were inventions originating in the minds of gospel writers who might even have employed the languages and ideas which they found in some non-Christian literature. But where is the proof?

Morris answers, "Though it is widely assumed that this procedure was rife in the ancient world little evidence can be found for it. That is to say, little evidence can be found that careful and serious writers practiced it."[59]

Morris goes on to quote A. W. Mosely from his *Historical Reporting in the Ancient World*:

> Several scholars have already studied this matter and the general conclusion has been

58. Schoenfield, *The Passover Plot,* pp. 220-221.
59. Morris, *Studies in the Fourth Gospel*, p. 68.

> that sometimes ancient historians felt at liberty to compose speeches for their reports. Even this is now being questioned. But our survey has shown that these same historians did not feel free to invent stories of past events. . . . Several writers (especially Herodotus, Thucydides, Polybius, Dionysius, Lucian, Cicero, and Josephus) had set out plainly the standards by which historical reports should be described as they happened.[60]

According to both Morris' and Mosely's research, the liberal view that men of antiquity were ready to invent speeches and events in order to bring out a truth is merely an assumption. Mosely is careful to say that ancient writers did not hesitate to compose speeches, when necessary, and put them into the mouths of historical characters, but that they did not regard themselves as having unlimited freedom in this matter, and that they were careful to make the speeches from reliable reports of what the original speakers were likely to have said. And he further makes the very important point that, while they composed speeches in this way, they did not compose stories of events. Thus Morris concludes that, "The widespread modern view that men of antiquity were quite ready to distort the facts if only they could bring out the truth, is not

60. Ibid., p. 69.

supported by the statements of the men themselves. It is simply assumed."[61]

Morris makes the interesting observation on ancient and modern writers relating to the matter of inventing speeches and events without any historical basis: "But only the second-rate did this (for that matter the second-rate in modern times are not exempt from guilt in this matter; but we do not therefore argue that this is standard practice)."[62]

To take some examples of second-rate writers from antiquity who invented speeches and events without historical basis and then to affirm that this was the way men wrote in the first century is not an accurate application of the material. The evidence showing us the established procedure makes it clear that such was not the way men normally wrote in the first century, says Morris.

The modern critical view has at its base a disrespect for the Scriptures and manifests, by its glib approach to them, an obvious prejudice against believing, which no amount of evidence can change. No other literary production has been so unfairly treated, especially in the face of so much established historical evidence.

Remember that the writers of the New Testament, when recording the claims and deeds of Jesus, asked us to believe that what they wrote was actually true—not theologically true, but his-

61. Ibid., p. 69.
62. Ibid., p. 69.

torically true. Their productions are written in the plain, easy-to-understand style of the historian, the space-time dimension. They have the sane and sober appearance of historical documents. If upon investigation, we find that their productions are not true as they affirmed, then let us denounce them as either lies or naive deceptions. But to build a theology upon inventions and then to ask men to believe that this is the way God communicates his eternal truths is nonsense—the product of unbelieving and distorted minds.

Liberalism Claims the Gospel Miracles Mean Something Else

What possible value could literature possess which falsely claimed to record the truth of God's intervention into the historical realm? Liberalism says that New Testament literature, though untrue historically, nevertheless has theological value—that back of the literary invention is theology. That this is accepted by many is seen in the references to it made in encyclopedic articles, which generally are looked to for facts. For example, The *Encyclopedia Americana* says:

> It is now widely agreed that a sign as John portrays it is neither a rent in the natural order nor an affront to man's higher intelligence, but a story-symbol of extraordinary penetration, comprehensiveness, and imaginative genius. The marriage feast at Cana

> (John 2:1-11) may serve as illustration: the water is Judaism, the mother is the faithful community in Israel, and the wine is the new life in Christ.[63]

But I raise the question, who is it that is "now widely agreed" with this sort of interpretation? Why, those who hold the modern view, of course. But to state without qualification that "it is now widely agreed," as if this were the general concensus, is untrue.

Another question must be raised: How do we know that John's account of the wedding feast miracle of changing water to wine is a story-symbol? You cannot get that idea from reading the Gospel of John. And how do we know that the interpretation given by the critic is the correct interpretation? And even if it is, how shall he prove it to us?

If one will read the gospel account of Jesus changing water into wine he will find no indication that the writer was telling a story which was to be symbolically interpreted. He will see that the writer asked us to believe that the event happened and that that was the reason we should believe on Jesus. Even later in the gospel (4:46-48), the same miracle is mentioned as a historical fact sufficient to have caused a nobleman from Capernaum, whose son was sick, to go to Cana to seek out Jesus that he might heal his son. This is not worthy of

63. Vol. XVI. p. 160, 1967 edition.

being called a story-symbol. Such an interpretation is pure conjecture without evidence, and in contradiction to the writer's stated intention for recording the incident.

John claimed to be an eyewitness of this event and insists that it actually happened in space and time just as he wrote it (19:35; 20:30-31). If it can be determined that this event was not historically true, then John must be convicted of lying. But the critic will not jeopardize his theology by admitting to a lie; he prefers to refer to the language as "extraordinary penetration" and "imaginative genius."

In his *Daily Study Bible,* Professor William Barclay illustrates this modern view of rejecting the gospel writer's statements as historical fact and telling us that they really mean something else. Commenting on Matthew's account of the virgin birth he says:

> The Virgin Birth is a doctrine which presents us with many difficulties; and it is a doctrine which our Church does not compel us to accept in the literal and physical sense. This is one of the doctrines on which the Church says that we have full liberty to come to our own belief and our own conclusion. At the moment we are concerned only to find out what this means to us.[64]

64. William Barclay, *The Gospel of Matthew,* Vol. 1, p. 10.

Professor Barclay brushes aside the inspired account of the virgin birth as though Matthew did not mean what he said, and then proceeds to ask, "What then does it mean to say that in the birth of Jesus the Holy Spirit of God is specially operative?" He explains that, "We must interpret it in the light of the Jewish idea of the Holy Spirit."[65] Barclay says that Matthew's account of the virgin birth is not the word of the Holy Spirit, but his own peculiar Jewish idea.

There are at least three fallacies between Matthew's statement of history and professor Barclay's comments. First, to read the account is to get the definite impression that Matthew wants us to believe that what he said is exactly what happened. This is clear from his introduction: "Now the birth of Jesus Christ was on this wise: When his mother Mary had been betrothed to Joseph, before they came together she was found with child of the Holy Spirit" (Matthew 1:18). The apostle Matthew does not leave us to speculate on the fact that Jesus was conceived supernaturally. He added the words of the heavenly messenger to Joseph: "That which is conceived in her is of the Holy Spirit" (Matthew 1:20). He explained that this Holy Spirit impregnation and consequent virgin birth was the fulfillment of the prophecy which was made by the Lord himself when he said through Isaiah, "Behold, a virgin shall conceive, and bear a

65. Ibid., p. 11.

son, and shall call his name Immanuel" (Isaiah 7:14). This is how the apostle, directed by the Holy Spirit, explained the prophetic meaning of the Lord's name, "which is, being interpreted, God with us" (Matthew 1:23).

Second, the virgin birth presents no problem whatsoever to those who regard the Scriptures to be historically reliable. If the virgin birth was an historic reality and Matthew wanted to tell us about it, could he have related it any clearer than he did? How can we determine what Matthew intended to say if he did not say what he meant?

Third, Barclay's statement that the Church does not compel us to interpret Matthew's account of the virgin birth in the literal and physical sense sets the word of God aside as authoritative and enthrones the Church, mere men, as the authority! What authority, then, could the Scriptures possibly have if the Church has the right to give us full liberty to come to our own belief? But the Church is not the authority in the Christian religion; that authority is resident in the written word of God (Matthew 28:18-20; John 12:48; 1 Corinthians 4:6; 14:37; 2 Thessalonians 2:15; 1 Peter 5:12; Revelation 20:12). The Church has no prerogative to release itself from believing what the Holy Spirit says to us in his word. Paul wrote, "Therefore he that rejecteth, rejecteth not man, but God, who giveth his Holy Spirit unto you" (1 Thessalonians 4:8).

Professor Barclay continues in his commentary on John's gospel to say that what the writer said is not just exactly true. His modernistic view of the resurrection of Lazarus once again asks us to believe that John's account means something other than what it appears to say. He begins by saying that the account in the other three gospels of people being raised from the dead can be explained by believing that the person raised was in a coma or a trance. From that point, he proceeds to say that in those gospels, there is no mention of the raising of Lazarus, and had Lazarus actually been raised, the other gospel writers would surely have mentioned it. Then, after relating four alternative explanations to the historical fact of the raising of Lazarus, he offers these words:

> We are in the end compelled to say that we do not know what happened at Bethany, but undoubtedly something tremendous did happen. . . . But we do know for certain the truth which this story teaches. . . . It does not really matter whether or not Jesus literally raised a corpse to life in a.d. 30, but it matters intensely that Jesus is the Resurrection and the Life for every man who is dead in sin and dead to God in a.d. 1955.[66]

Barclay tries to explain the resurrection of Lazarus in a totally nonliteral manner saying that

66. William Barclay, *The Gospel of John,* Vol . II pp. 118-120.

it is to be understood in the spiritual new birth. But isn't that making something of the story totally other than what John said? A lot of us are wondering just how Jesus could possibly be meaningful to us in this century as the resurrection and the life if he did not in fact raise someone from the dead in the first century.

Personally, I am quite fond of Professor Barclay, if not his theology. His schedule was not too busy to include me and my traveling companion, Ed Myers, in a prearranged meeting at his home in Glasgow in the early part of April 1970. I had written earlier from India requesting an interview to discuss critical questions of the fourth gospel and kept our appointment on my return trip. It was there that I asked him to explain why he believed the account of the empty tomb in John 20 was of a historical nature but that the account of Lazarus in chapter 11 was not. His immediate answer was, "It is not recorded in Mark." That was the occasion of an interesting observation in as much as the professor makes much of John's historical account of the grave cloths in the tomb which is not recorded in Mark either! Do we not have a right to expect at least consistency in our theology?

The modernistic view of the four gospels contradicts the very language of the gospel writers themselves. What should be evident is that the gospels are either historically true or they are not. If they do not relate the literal truth they say they do, then they offer us nothing for a sure foundation for a present theology or a future hope for eternal life.

THE VALUE OF THE CRITICAL VIEW

If the modern view of Scripture is at all valuable to us, surely those values can be objectively stated. Is this view valuable historically? Do we now have more information of the historical facts of Christianity's origin and spread? Do we have more information concerning the people of those days or the response of those people to the gospel? Let the historian A. M. Sherwin-White answer:

> It is astonishing that while Graeco-Roman historians have been growing in confidence, the twentieth century study of the gospel narratives, starting from no less promising material, has taken so gloomy a turn in the development of form-criticism that the more advanced exponents of it apparently maintain, so far as an amateur can understand the matter, that the historical Christ is unknowable and the history of his mission cannot be written. This seems very curious.[67]

It is curious that historians of Greece and Rome grow continually more confident of the culture, conditions, and life-style of those ancient nations through the materials they have, while the higher

67. *Roman Society and Roman Law in the New Testament*, Oxford, 1963, p. 187.

criticism, working with materials as reliable as the gospels, grows more uncertain of the historical events that surrounded Jesus. They have only cluttered the picture. Modernism has taken the garment of Christianity and has cut it to shreds, leaving us mere patches which do not fit into any pattern. Of what value are these rags? J. V. Langmead Casserley sums up the modern view quite well in the following words:

> From within the biblical tradition we must insist and confidently expect that the more profoundly and validly we understand and interpret the Bible, the greater the religious depth with which it will challenge and speak to us. It is precisely here that modern biblical scholarship has proved itself so insipid and unstimulating. We are confronted with the paradox of a way of studying the word of God out of which no word of God ever seems to come, with an imposing modern knowledge of the Bible which seems quite incapable of saying anything biblical or thinking biblically.[68]

Is the value of the modern view of the gospels objective? Can we know what God through Jesus said and taught and required of us? Can we, by the modern approach to the New Testament, know, that having done what God said, that we are saved? And can we know it so certainly that we can share it with others whom we know, through bibli-

68. *Toward a Theology of History,* London, 1965, p. 116.

cal teaching, are lost without that gospel? The answer from the modernistic camp is no. Nothing seems to be certain from this viewpoint except that the Bible does not say what it means. This is due to the approach which the modernist takes to the historical framework in which the gospel accounts are set and the doctrine which takes its rise from it—that which claims to be history is not history, the events described did not really happen, the claims of Jesus were not really made! This modern approach is totally subjective. It has enthroned religious subjectivism and totally abandoned the authority of the Scriptures.

The modern view of the New Testament appears to be neither valid nor valuable. It is prejudice which is perpetrated against historic Christianity in the sophisticated garb of scholarship and the respectability of so-called theology. In the final analysis, it is not theology at all, according to the actual meaning of that term. It is unbelief, pure and simple. It is not worthy of being called scholarship when the facts are continually brushed aside for philosophical presuppositions, and when it refuses to consider bonafide evidence and draw conclusions from that basis. The critical view is in fact not so much a view of the Bible as it is the kind of opposition to the truth against which Paul warned us: "O Timothy, guard that which is committed unto thee, turning away from the profane babblings and oppositions of the knowledge which is falsely so called; which some professing have erred concerning the faith" (1 Timothy 6:20-21).

The modern critical view of the New Testament is worthy of no more consideration than the time it takes to warn men of its destructive nature that they may stand clear of its danger.

Second Appendix

The Objective Nature of the Historic Christian Gospel

12

The Objective Nature of the Historic Christian Gospel

It is a tragic, if interesting, quirk of the present era that Bible things are being discussed and conclusions are being reached without any reference to the Bible.

—Ed Wharton

God has worked out his plan for human redemption in history. Because of its once-for-all, never-to-be-repeated nature, history must be communicated to today's man in understandable language. The past comes to us only through testimony. Only words with plain and definite meanings can convey to our minds and hearts the exact nature of that redemption which God accomplished in space and time. Our salvation was provided by the great Christ events of the first century; but in modern times, justification by faith comes only through hearing those historic events. Since they will never be repeated, we must hear them in order to believe them. That requires an understandable communication from God, and that is what the New Testament is.

The Objective Nature of the Word of God

In the first century, there were men who were guided by the Holy Spirit to speak the gospel in words that were easy to understand and definite in meaning. Luke said that on the day the Holy Spirit came to the apostles, "they were filled with the Holy Spirit, and began to speak with other tongues, as the Spirit gave them utterance" (Acts 2:4). They began speaking of the wonderful works of God throughout history in order to gain the attention of the crowd (2:11-13), and then they proclaimed Christ crucified and raised. The clarity of the message was unmistakable. Luke's statement that they were pricked in their heart and the cry of the multitude, "Brethren, what shall we do?" (2:37), elicited from Peter the clear terms of pardon which saving faith required (2:38). Then stated Luke, "With many other words he testified, and exhorted them, saying, Save yourselves from this crooked generation," and three thousand Jews stepped forward for baptism (2:40-41). There was nothing in the word of the apostles that left the required response of the multitude to guesswork. They were led by plain words to believe in the resurrected Christ, and, following salvation, "they continued stedfastly in the apostles' teaching" (2:42). Later, the Roman centurion, Cornelius, was told to send to Peter, "who shall speak unto thee words whereby thou shalt be saved" (Acts 11:14). This gospel communication was not generated by human impulse or by existentialistic experience. It was communicated by the medium of understandable words.

In Paul's great effort to correct the problem of division, which intellectual pride and glorying in men caused in the church at Corinth, he explained that their salvation was not due to the golden oratory of Apollos or to the powerful presence of Peter or Paul, but it was due to knowable words of the Spirit. As Paul said, "But we [the apostles] received, not the spirit of the world, but the spirit which is from God; that we might know the things that were freely given to us of God. Which things also we speak, not in words which man's wisdom teacheth, but which the Spirit teacheth" (1 Corinthians 2:12-13).

God has never left it for people to learn of gospel truth by subjective interpretations of their own personal experiences. Jeremiah pronounced the absolute inability of men and women to go right, even when they try, without God as their counselor, when he said, "O Jehovah, I know that the way of man is not in himself; it is not in man that walketh to direct his steps" (Jeremiah 10:23). The apostle

Paul expressed the same truth when he wrote, "For seeing that in the wisdom of God the world through its wisdom knew not God, it was God's good pleasure through the foolishness of the preaching to save them that believe" (1 Corinthians 1:21). All the wisdom of mankind combined cannot produce the knowledge of salvation's gospel; only the word of God can do that. Salvation is through believing in Jesus as Lord and Saviour, but "belief cometh of hearing, and hearing by the word of Christ" (Romans 10:17). The gospel of salvation is a clear and distinct word.

While some of the acts of God throughout history could have been easily recognized for their supernatural character, without written testimony, we could know nothing of them nor could they have been properly perceived and explained as redemptive in nature. God had to tell us, for example, that the purpose of Israel as a nation in the earth was to serve his purpose in bringing the Saviour into the world. He had to interpret for us the redemptive meaning of Christ's sinless life, his death on the cross, and his resurrection. Neither these historic facts nor their redemptive meaning could be known to us today without the written word and without the clarity of the meaning of those words.

God has produced a written testimony of his redemptive historical activities in words which can be understood. He has preserved those historical space-time events and what they mean for all time to come. Through his written word, he continues to reveal his redemptive plan in modern times.

Corruptive Influences of Religious Subjectivism Upon the Word of God

The word of God has always had its enemies; they have always been about the same. From the Jews have come the legalists, who, because they understood neither law nor grace, attempted to bind the law of Moses upon saved Gentiles, thus nullifying the grace of God (Galatians 2:21). From among the Gentiles have come the religious mystics and speculators who have substituted philosophy and human wisdom for the plain meaning of God's word (Colossians 2:8-10). It is this latter method and its modern manifestation that I want to deal with in this final chapter.

Paul identified the method which our arch enemy would employ to corrupt the plain and absolute meaning of the saving words of God when he said, "But I fear, lest by any means, as the serpent beguiled Eve in his craftiness, your minds should be corrupted from the simplicity and the purity that is toward Christ" (2 Corinthians 11:3). Satan's method of corrupting modern minds is identified with his initially successful effort upon Eve. He lied to her about the word of God. God had plainly stated that they could eat freely of all the trees in the garden except for one particular tree. Of the fruit of that tree he said clearly, "in the day that thou eatest thereof thou shalt surely die" (Genesis 2:17). But Satan, intending to murder the entire human race, lied to the woman saying, "Ye shall not surely die" (Genesis 3:4). He corrupted her mind by lying to her about the word of God. By destroying her respect for the word, he destroyed her. His modern method is the same—to use men who appear to be ministers of the word, but who in reality corrupt the plain meaning of its language (2 Corinthians 11:14-15).

In the preceding chapter, we saw a modern manifestation of this method to corrupt men's minds against the word. Modern liberalism has attempted to cloud the plain meaning of God's word by telling us that it is not historically trustworthy, that it is filled with mythical stories, and that we are too far removed from what actually happened to know anything for sure about the true nature and life of Christ. The effect has been telling. Suspicion covers the Bible in the minds of many who have never thought it necessary to investigate for themselves.

The present wave of religious subjectivism produces the same alienation from the authority of the word by seeking to find another, sometimes mystical or occultic, meaning in the Scriptures—other than its apparent and plain meaning. Subjectivism seeks to bring us to faith in Christ by appealing to modern religious experiences apart from knowledge of the Scripture rather than by appealing to the historic testimony for the resurrection. This modern method bypasses the New Testament by claiming guidance from the Holy Spirit. As proof, the Lord's statement to the apostles is quoted: "Howbeit when he, the Spirit of truth, is come, he shall guide you into all the truth" (John 16:13). It seems to make no difference that in the context Jesus is stating that this particular gift of the Spirit was promised to the apostles who were to share the word with us by preaching (1 Peter 1:12) and by the written word (Ephesians 3:3-4; 1 Peter 5:12).

It is a tragic, if interesting, quirk of the present religious era that Bible things are being discussed and conclusions are being reached without any reference to the Bible. It appears as if people are pooling their Bible ignorance in the name of Jesus and calling it Christianity! Evidence for the living Christ, we are told, is supposed to be found in the joyful feelings of the heart. This is expressed in the church hymn:

> He lives! He lives!
> You ask me how I know he lives:
> He lives within my heart.

However, it is a practical impossibility to know whether or not Jesus is presently living by an appeal to the swelling emotions of the human heart. The feeling of joy in Christianity is the result of faith, not proof of the thing believed. The only way known to man to confirm the living

Christ today is by an appeal to the historical testimony of the apostles. The testimony of the Holy Spirit to the living Lord is not in the feelings which he produces, but in the written word which he revealed and had written.

Redemption Revealed in Words

Both the purpose and methodology of the Holy Spirit in modern times is the same as it was in the first century: to bring men to faith in the crucified and risen Jesus by the means of the plain and definitive words which he gave to the apostles. The Spirit's work is not mystical. He does not leave it to men to wonder whether he is guiding them. His work of revelation and redemption, both then and now, is accomplished through the medium of the words which he imparted to the apostles and prophets in the first century. Our faith in Christ today and all of our instructions in the Christian system are due to that apostolic word which has been preserved in written form.

Let's consider that methodology for our own time.

The Promised Work of the Holy Spirit to the Apostles

Jesus prepared the apostles for their work of preaching when he told them that the Holy Spirit would guide them in their testimony. He said, "He shall teach you all things, and bring to your remembrance all that I said unto you," and, "when he, the Spirit of truth, is come, he shall guide you into all the truth: for he shall not speak from himself; but what things soever he shall hear, these shall he speak" (John 14:26; 16:13). This promise was made only to the apostles, not to us today. If it was a promise for the church today, we would not need a New Testament. Remember that Jesus' prayer, which he prayed for us today, was for those who believe on him through the apostles' word (John 17:20). Their word was declared by Christ to be the basis of our present-day faith in him. The apostles received the word from the Holy Spirit who then gave it to us (1 Corinthians 2:10-13; 11:23). Our faith today is due to the testimony which the Holy Spirit gave to those apostles.

The Completed Work of the Holy Spirit Upon the Apostles

The claim of the apostles was that the Holy Spirit did the work which Jesus promised when he revealed the mystery of God's eternal purpose. Paul wrote that God's eternal redemptive purpose for humanity was a mystery until apostolic times. He tells us that this wisdom of God, foreordained before the worlds for our glorification, was hidden from the minds of men until it was revealed to the apostles by the Holy Spirit (1 Corinthians 2:7; Ephesians 1:9-11; 3:10-11) and was written in plain words which could be read and understood. Paul laid it down with clarity that, "by revelation was made known unto me the mystery, as I wrote before in few words, whereby, when ye read, ye can perceive my understanding in the mystery of Christ; which in other generations was not made known unto the sons of men, as it hath now been revealed unto his holy apostles and prophets in the Spirit" (Ephesians 3:3-5). The apostles received the revelation of the gospel from the Holy Spirit and wrote it for us in words which can be understood. This is how the Spirit produces faith and salvation today, by the written words he gave to the apostles. As Paul said, "Belief cometh of hearing, and hearing by the word of Christ" (Romans 10:17). Our belief today is produced by the words of the apostles—the same word which produced the same faith in the first century.

Peter echoes the promise of Jesus that the Holy Spirit would teach the apostles all things when he wrote that "his divine power [the Holy Spirit] hath granted unto us all things that pertain unto life and godliness, through the knowledge of him that called us" (2 Peter 1:3). And the apostle John, having delivered all those things to the church, wrote to remind them that because of the coming of the Holy Spirit to the apostles, they knew all things (1 John 2:20), and added, "I have not written unto you because ye know not the truth, but because ye know it" (2:21). A few verses down he wrote, "let that abide in you which ye heard from the beginning. If that which ye heard from the beginning abide in you, ye also shall abide in the Son, and in the Father." What they had heard from the beginning was the word of the gospel; it was the same things Paul and Peter wrote that the Holy Spirit had revealed to them. They all were saying the same thing—that because of the coming of the Holy Spirit to the apostles, we now can hear and believe in Christ, and that faith which their word produced is to be preserved and honored above all other words.

In Peter's first letter, he claimed that Jesus' promise that the Holy Spirit would come to the apostles and guide them into all gospel truth had been fulfilled (1 Peter 1:12). He closed his letter by saying, "I have written unto you briefly, exhorting, and testifying that this is the true grace of God: stand ye fast therein" (1 Peter 5:12). Peter said the Spirit revealed it, that he wrote it, and we are to stand fast in it. That is how the Holy Spirit directs us today—by his written word. Paul stated it clearly, "If any man thinketh himself to be a prophet, or spiritual, let him take knowledge of the things which I write unto you, that they are the commandment of the Lord" (1 Corinthians 14:37). When Paul wrote to the church at Thessalonica to "hold the traditions which ye were taught, whether by word, or by epistle of ours" (2 Thessalonians 2:15), he was saying that the written word—his epistle—was the authority in Christianity. When the resurrected Lord used the apostle John to write letters to the seven churches of Asia, he used a formula to close out each letter, saying, "He that hath an ear, let him hear what the Spirit saith to the churches" (Revelation 2 and 3). The Holy Spirit spoke through those letters. While he directed John to address each letter to the particular needs of each of the different churches, they were exhorted to hear what was in each one of the letters as though each one had been addressed to all the churches. "He that hath an ear, let him hear what the Spirit saith," that is, in those letters. That is how the Holy Spirit communicated then, and that is how he communicates today—in those same letters which we call the New Testament.

The Apostles Had a Word Ministry

Jesus commissioned his apostles to go into all the world and preach the gospel to the whole creation (Mark 16:15). He gave them a ministry that required them to speak words. When the Holy Spirit came to them, he enabled them to fulfill that commission. Paul spoke of this ministry which the Spirit brought to them when he said, "But all things are of God, who reconciled us to himself through Christ, and gave unto us the ministry of reconciliation; to wit, that God was in Christ reconciling the world unto himself, not reckoning unto them their trespasses, and having committed unto us the word of reconciliation" (2 Corinthians 5:18-19).

First he stated that God gave them the ministry of reconciliation. The point is that God gave the apostles a word ministry—a ministry of words to speak which would bring men to faith in Christ and therefore to a reconciliation with God.

The Work of the Holy Spirit in Current Times

Does the Holy Spirit operate in our current times? If so, how does he work to bring men to Christ? How does he direct the affairs of his people? How does he change the lives of men? As a final consideration, I want to answer these questions under the following heads:

1. How the Holy Spirit saves today

"Verily, verily, I say unto thee, Except one be born of water and the Spirit, he cannot enter into the kingdom of God" (John 3:5). Paul wrote that God "saved us, through the washing of regeneration and renewing of the Holy Spirit" (Titus 3:5). These clear statements reveal that the Spirit is engaged in bringing about a spiritual new birth. But Paul also wrote to the Corinthians that he was their spiritual father, in that he had brought them to Christ, as he said, "in Christ Jesus I begat you through the gospel" (1 Corinthians 4:15). How, then, is the spiritual renewing process brought about—by the Holy Spirit, as earlier stated, or by the gospel? Actually, it is not an either/or matter. We are saved by faith in Christ. Faith comes by the word of Christ which the Holy Spirit revealed to the apostles. They preached the word and it produced saving faith. Spiritual renewal is a process:

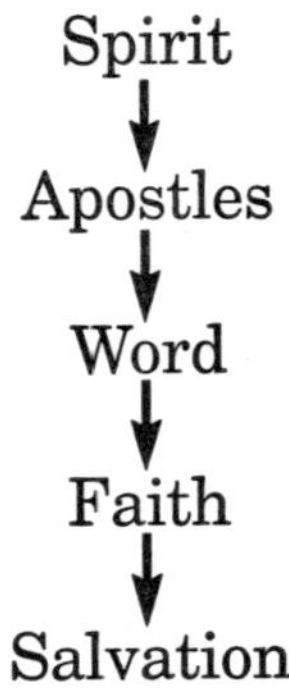

Peter wrote that Christians had "been begotten again, not of corruptible seed, but of incorruptible, through the word of God, which liveth and abideth" (1 Peter 1:23). James wrote the same thing when he said that God had "of his own will brought us forth by the word of truth" (James 1:18). The rebirth in all these references is attributed to the Holy Spirit, to the gospel, and to the word of God. The clear and distinctive pronouncement of the Spirit himself is that he saves us through the agency of his word.

2. How the Holy Spirit leads his people today

"But I say, Walk by the Spirit, and ye shall not fulfill the lust of the flesh . . . But if ye are led by the Spirit, ye are not under the law" (Galatians 5:16, 18); "For as many as are led by the Spirit of God, these are sons of God" (Romans 8:14). With no more instruction than these few statements, it might seem that the Christian has a special conversational acquaintance with the Holy Spirit by which he is personally guided. This position is not without adherents. But the Spirit leads the children of God in their Christian life as objectively as he led them to faith in Christ. Paul said, "We through the Spirit by faith wait for the hope of righteousness" (Galatians 5:5). What Christians do by the Spirit, they do by faith. And I would remind you once again that faith comes by hearing the word of Christ. This agrees with Paul's statement that "we walk by faith" (2 Corinthians 5:7). Now, as in the first century, the Holy Spirit leads men by his word into faith in Jesus Christ and into a fruitful Christian life. The process can be expressed this way:

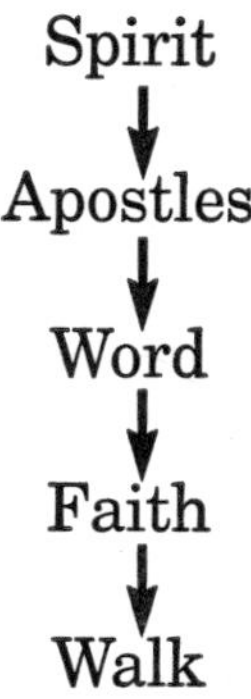

This is what Jesus commissioned the apostles to do: "teaching them to observe all things whatsoever I commanded you" (Matthew 28:20). When we know what God wants us to do through the word of the Holy Spirit, we are enabled to know those who are being led by the Spirit. In this way, we can identify the children of God. As John said, "In this the children of God are manifest, and the children of the devil: whosoever doeth not righteousness is not of God" (1 John 3:10).

This comment on the Spirit's objective guidance for the children of God does not touch upon the subject of the providential guidance of the children of God. The two must not be confused. God's providential control of the affairs of people and nations to bring about his own desired ends cannot be determined subjectively. Whether God has employed the ministration of angels (Hebrews 1:14) to accomplish his purpose, or some other means, cannot be determined by any personal experience. We are taught in the Scriptures to believe that God is at work in the earth, that he answers our supplications for the sick (James 5:14-18), that he gives grace to his people to assist them in time of trial (Hebrews 4:14-16), that he hears our prayer for the lost (Romans 10:1-3), and that he extends his great might over the nations of the earth in behalf of his church to accomplish her task of world evangelism (1 Timothy 2:1-5; Ephesians 3:20-21). But no Christian could ever *prove* that

God answered his prayer by either the Holy Spirit's activity or by angels or by some other means. Our knowledge of God's present space-time activity comes only from his own revelation of that fact in the Scriptures. We could not know it otherwise.

3. How the Holy Spirit bears his fruit today

"But the fruit of the Spirit is love, joy, peace, longsuffering, kindness, goodness, faithfulness, meekness, self-control" (Galatians 5:22-23). We must not be so naive as to equate every good feeling with what the Holy Spirit has done. The Bible has many warnings against false doctrines. History tells us that people have believed false doctrines, mistaking them for truth, and have rejoiced in the belief that they were saved. But the Holy Spirit did not produce that joy—false doctrine did.

It is in the revelation of the good news of Christ crucified and raised that the Holy Spirit produces his fruit of joy in those that believe and accept salvation. The other fruits of the Spirit are also produced by the Spirit's word, like faithfulness: since faith is the product of the word of God, the standard of Christian faithfulness can be discerned by a knowledge of that word. Thus the process can be expressed in the following:

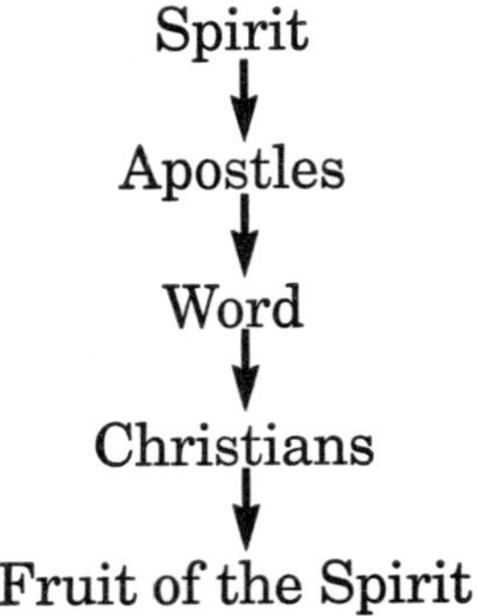

It is through the written word of God that the Holy Spirit saves us, guides us, and bears his fruit.

Man's Response to an Objective Faith

We can think of the Spirit—apostles—word—faith—salvation process another way: we can think of it as salvation by education. Inherent in the great commission which Jesus gave to his apostles was an educational process, "Go ye therefore, and make disciples of all nations, baptizing them into the name of the Father and of the Son and of the Holy Spirit, teaching them to observe all things whatsoever I commanded you" (Matthew 28:19-20). The apostles went forth making disciples by teaching the gospel of Christ. But men and women must respond by listening and learning. During his ministry, Jesus referred to this same process. He said, "Come unto me, all ye that labor and are heavy laden, and I will give you rest. Take my yoke upon you, and learn of me" (Matthew 11:28-29). Note that the "come unto me . . . and learn of me" educational process is present in this great invitation. At another time, Jesus explained the process by which all men would be enabled to come to him, "No man can come to me, except the Father that sent me draw him: and I will raise him up in the last day. It is written in the prophets, And they shall all be taught of God. Every one that hath heard from the Father, and hath learned, cometh unto me" (John 6:44-45). Belief in Christ is the result of educating people to the historic facts of the space-time gospel. When the gospel is taught and people learn it, they can answer his invitation and come to him by faith.

The entire thrust of this book has been to present the historical nature of the evidence for the Christian religion in order to provide modern men and women with an objective faith, that they might respond to that invitation to salvation. While religious subjectivism says, in essence, "I know because of what I feel," the objective Christian system says, "I feel because of what I know." When we know because of his understandable word what God has done for us in history, when we know what he promised to faithful believers, when we know what he requires of us, and then do it, we will know of our saved relationship; and the joyous feeling that comes from knowing that our eternal destiny has been sealed by the living Lord will naturally flood our hearts and souls. This is beautifully illustrated in the conversion of the Ethiopian eunuch, who learned of Christ through Philip the evangelist, was brought to belief and baptism and then "went on his way rejoicing" (Acts 8:26-39). He was taught of God, he learned of Christ, and responded by faith. Then knowing that he was saved, he rejoiced in his salvation. This joy and rejoicing will continue to be the result of man's response to an objective faith.

Christianity offers to all people at all times a confirmation by historical evidence that Jesus Christ is the resurrected son of God and provides us with an objective avenue of response to his offer of salvation. Today's man who desires to have knowledge of who he is and where he is going can find his answer in the totally reliable pages of the New Testament of our Lord and Saviour Jesus Christ.